YOUR GOD,
MY GOD,
OUR
GOD

© 2026 – 1st edition

ISBN: 978-1-948109-48-2
LCCN: 2026934348

UNITED STATES SPIRITIST COUNCIL (USSC)
www.spiritist.us

INTERNATIONAL SPIRITIST COUNCIL (CEI)
Av. L2 Norte – Q. 603 – Conjunto F (SGAN)
70830-030 – Brasília (DF) – Brazil

Texts follow the spelling and syntactic conventions of the authors' countries of origin.

Cover Design, Graphic Project, and Layout:
Sara Barros

Project Coordinator (English Edition/Translation):
Jussara Pretti Korngold

YOUR GOD,
MY GOD,
OUR GOD

Anthology of Spiritist Reflections on God,
from scientific, philosophical, and religious perspectives,
originally published in the *Revue Spirite* between
October 2020 and July 2021.

YOUR GOD, MY GOD, OUR GOD

ALUIZIO FERREIRA ELIAS

ARISMAR LÉON PEREIRA

DÉCIO IANDOLI JR.

EULÁLIA BUENO

HUMBERTO SCHUBERT COELHO

JOSÉ LUIZ PEIXINHO

LAUDELINO RISSO

RAÚL TEIXEIRA E ALESSANDRO DE PAULA

REJANE PLANER

SÍLVIA ALMEIDA

SIMÃO PEDRO LIMA

SUELY CALDAS SCHUBERT

TABLE OF CONTENTS

Revue Spirite *web page*

As noted by the Spirit Emmanuel, in a profound and enlightened vision, God sustains life, endows intelligence, illumines through reason, nourishes with love, inspires circumstances, creates possibilities, grants the gift of speech, spreads resources, suggests goodness, sends what we are capable of receiving, and establishes free thought.

Using the resources that the Creator bestows upon the creature, twelve authors reflected upon God—God's Existence, Nature, and Manifestation. They drew upon the time and nature of their present experience in matter, upon their intelligence and reason. Nourished by God's love and invited to exercise the gift of written expression, they practiced free thought and applied the best they were capable of receiving and conceiving.

Thus, this anthology brings together twelve Spiritist reflections on God, published throughout the first year of the new edition of the *Revue Spirite,* founded by Allan Kardec in 1858 and today the official organ of the International Spiritist Council.

Through these reflections, may the reader find a new opportunity and a meaningful pretext to delve into contemplation of God, and, in an ever deeper and more personal reflection, to discover oneself and to find God. For, *"Everywhere we will find the creature associated with the Creator in the occurrences of Creation. Divine Providence and human cooperation always arise together (...) from God comes the gift, and from Humanity flows its application."* *

Revue Spirite Team

*XAVIER, Francisco C. (Emmanuel, Spirit). 2008. "God and Us", in the book *Encontro Marcado.* Brasília: FEB.

Rejane Planer is an electrical and nuclear engineer, with a background in nuclear physics and a master's degree in nuclear engineering from the Military Institute of Engineering (IME) in Rio de Janeiro, Brazil. Since 1989, she has lived and worked in Austria. Now retired from the International Atomic Energy Agency (IAEA), she served for 27 years in various positions related to nuclear energy and nuclear safety.

An accomplished writer and poet, she contributes articles to several Brazilian Spiritist magazines, including *Presença Espírita, Revista Internacional do Espiritismo, Momento Espírita,* and *Reformador*. She is also the co-founder and vice president of the Allan Kardec Spiritist Studies Association (*Verein für Spiritistische Studien Allan Kardec*) in Vienna, Austria.

Website: www.rejaneplaner.org

In this article, we have use God to name the Omnipresent Creator and god for the mythological gods of antiquity. We also treated God as neutral but kept excerpts as in the original.

YOUR GOD, MY GOD, OUR GOD

REJANE PLANER

It is challenging to write about God.

How can one define the indefinable? How can we explain the gratitude we feel for life and for the beauty of nature that shines around us? Or the humility that overtakes us when we gaze at the starry sky, pointing to the existence of countless stars and, possibly, innumerable other worlds?

Indeed, we perceive the omnipresent Presence of God[1] when we marvel at the wonders of creation, for God is in everything—especially in the eternal cycle of life and death, where life perpetually renews itself. We are with God when we awaken in the morning, grateful for the gift of being alive. We also become aware of the Divine Presence when we meditate and connect with our inner Self—the Spirit we are—and with Creation itself, in a profound mystical experience that arises from immense gratitude for the privilege of existing.

And so, we ask: What is this God whom we perceive within ourselves and in all that is visible or invisible around us? This was also Allan Kardec's first question to the spiritual benefactors who guided him in the codification of Spiritism. The answer was:

"God is the Supreme Intelligence, the First Cause of all things." (*The Spirits' Book*, Kardec, 1857, q.1)

1 In this article, we have use God to name the Omnipresent Creator and god for the mythological gods of antiquity. We also treated God as neutral but kept excerpts as in the original.

How can we comprehend this Supreme Intelligence—this immeasurable Force that creates all beings and all things, and grants us the opportunity to experience life repeatedly until we learn that to live is to love, and that God's Law is Love?

Faced with our own smallness, we can only agree with Kardec, who so beautifully concludes in the introduction to *The Spirits' Book* that humanity may conceive of God in different ways and attribute to the Divine various qualities and names.

"Nevertheless, it is always God." (*The Spirits' Book*, Kardec, 1857, Introduction, §11)

That is, God remains incomprehensible to the evolutionary stage in which we presently find ourselves.

Truly understanding God is hard, but we can perceive God's presence within and acknowledge Its Presence in the Creation. Nevertheless, everyone feels God in different ways during its evolutionary journey.

God in human thinking

The belief in a superior and unknown force—God—is inherent to the development of humankind.

Primitive humans, unable to comprehend the forces of nature, nonetheless recognized their power and the threats they posed to survival. Thus, they associated these forces with deities.

The goddess of fertility was engraved in statues of female figures and cave paintings from the Paleolithic period[2] (35,000 B.C.). Birth was one of the great mysteries of those times.

2 The Palaeolithic period covers from 2.7 million years to 10,000 B.C. Human beings survived in a hostile nature, with simple habits and techniques; they already knew fire, but agriculture had not yet appeared.

The Neolithic period (from 8,000 BC to 5,000 BC) marks the beginning of agriculture and also the rise of nature worship. The fury of storms and other natural phenomena reflected instinctive human emotions such as anger, vengeance, hatred, and aggression. Consequently, many deities embodying these traits were revered during this era of magical thought.

Later, the ancient polytheistic civilizations worshiped anthropomorphic gods who mirrored human personalities. The Greco-Roman civilization was defined by its mythological pantheon of gods and heroes who lived out marvelous adventures—among them Hercules, Oedipus, Theseus, and Perseus. In the Americas, the Mayans and Aztecs venerated a central cosmological god alongside various secondary deities. In Asia, beliefs emerged in a Supreme Being as well as in intermediary spirits, celestial gods, and deities associated with the forces of nature.

In the Occident, the belief in one God emerged in Judaism and Zoroastrianism[3] and later, in Christianity and Islam. In the Orient, religious philosophies such as Hinduism, Buddhism, and Taoism encompass a diverse number of philosophical and spiritual systems with their own gods and rituals in distinct lines of thought of the Western religions.

Early monotheism also had an anthropomorphic character typical of the creature's egocentric nature, who perceive the world revolving around its interests. Jesus marked a new era and introduced a new conception of God. With Jesus, God is no longer the implacable, rancorous, and vindictive god. God loses its human characteristics to become a loving father, "the great and good God who is honored not by the form or ceremony, but by the sincere, heartfelt thought. He is no more the God to be feared, but the God to be loved." (KARDEC 1868, 21)

3 Zoroastrianism has its roots in Zoroaster or Zarathustra that presumably lived in the 20th century BC. Zoroastrianism was the religion of the Persian empire when under Cyro the Great as per historical records dating from the fifth century B.C.

> The understanding of God has slowly changed over the past two millennia. While some people still remain in stages of magical thinking, others broaden their horizons through the development of reason and reasoning. As presented by Kardec:
>
> "God being the pivot of all religious beliefs, the base of all civilizations, the character of all religions conforms to the idea they give of God. Those which make him vindictive and cruel think they honor him by acts of cruelty, by butcheries and tortures; those who make him a partial and jealous God are intolerant, over-scrupulous in forms, according as they believe in him to be more or less tainted with weaknesses and human errors." (Kardec, 1868, 21)

Learning is a gradual process that requires changes in behaviors and beliefs already engraved in the individual's unconscious. Consequently, even today some people bring God into the sphere of daily interests and worship a superior being conceptually similar to humankind, while others have developed a reasoned faith in the Creator, and still others deny the existence of God altogether.

For many, belief in God is a matter of faith. Yet, what kind of faith is this?

Faith and the belief in God

The word *faith* can be understood as trust in something, or, in a religious sense, as belief in a higher power or in God.

When faith in a superior force develops without questioning or reasoning, it may be rooted in fear and foster unbounded trust, for in such cases emotion rules rather than reason. This type of faith is characteristic of those who believe blindly. Unable to rationalize their beliefs, they become biased and fanatical, internalizing a faith of the absurd that can lead to extreme actions in the name of a God not understood but accepted without reflection.

Blind faith—sometimes exacerbated by socioeconomic and cultural factors—has often prompted reckless attitudes and thoughtless aggressions that have left deep scars on individuals and on humanity as a whole. The persecution of Christians, the religious wars, the Inquisition, the persecution of the Jewish people, and contemporary acts of terrorism are but a few examples of such wounds.

Faith grounded in an anthropomorphic concept of God still persists today. Blind faith continues to influence immature minds that attempt to bargain with God in pursuit of emotional or material satisfaction, or that assume postures and actions in the name of divine will, without truly understanding what God is or the spiritual reality of life.

In *The Gospel According to Spiritism* (1866), Allan Kardec linked faith with humility, knowledge, and trust in God. By recognizing their smallness before the grandeur of Creation, the individual reverently identifies as part of that Creation. The creature then perceives that everything in the Universe moves according to Divine Laws and gradually begins to strive to live in harmony with them. As Kardec wrote:

> "True faith is linked to humility; those who possess it place greater confidence in God than in themselves, for they know they are but simple instruments of the Divine Will and can do nothing without God." (Kardec, 1866, p. 202)

As the individual evolves, consciousness unfolds as well, leading the person to seek understanding of oneself and the world through reasoning. The human being aspires to acquire knowledge and to unravel the mysteries of existence: *Where did I come from? Where am I going? What is the purpose of life?*

Consequently, the individual develops rational faith—a faith that reflects, analyzes, and strives to comprehend the reality of life, recognizing the Creator through His creation. For such individuals, the intellect, when united with the profound feeling of awareness of one's place within Creation, becomes a sacred instrument for approaching the understanding of the incomprehensible.

God in scientific thinking

It is often assumed that science focuses on describing how the physical Universe operates, leaving the question of what created this Universe to philosophers, theologians, or to metaphysics.

However, the philosophers of antiquity were also scientists—mathematicians, physicists, chemists—researchers dedicated not only to uncovering the mysteries of nature and formulating theories and laws to explain the functioning of the physical world, but also to seeking answers to the fundamental questions of human existence.

Pythagoras[4] (*c.* sixth century BC) created mathematics as a system of thought based on deductive evidence, including the famous Pythagorean theorem, and made other scientific discoveries. He influenced Western thinking from Greek philosophy (e.g. Plato) to the Middle Ages (e.g. St. Augustine, St. Thomas Aquinas) and to modern times. Plato (4th - 5th century BC), philosopher and mathematician, discovered the inductive reasoning, laying the foundations of Western philosophy and science. Aristotle (4th century BC) contributed to a wide range of disciplines covering the most

4 The Pythagorean school was widespread in antiquity and influenced esoteric schools of an initiatory character.

varied fields of human and exact sciences. He developed the principle of logic and reasoning and heavily influenced human thought until the Middle Ages.

Since antiquity, Western science and philosophy have held hands, but they were also tied to the Church's thinking. The philosopher-scientists[5] influenced by Aristotelian philosophy did not make experiments as in today's science. They observed the events and made conclusions but, in general, did not use mathematics to develop their theories. Galileo[6] (1564-1642) broke this status *quo* by introducing mathematics into Aristotle's empiricism and, therefore, is considered by many as the father of the scientific method.

René Descartes (1596–1650), the French mathematician, physicist, and philosopher, gave rise to the doctrine of mind–matter dualism and introduced the mechanistic view of life. Descartes offered a new vision of the natural world—the world of matter—distinct from the realm of spirit or mind. This separation led scientists to study the material world through its fundamental properties and laws, perceiving it as an immense mechanism—*the universe as a great machine.*

Descartes also analyzed the concept of perfection, concluding that it could not originate from the senses but from reason. As an idea cannot arise from nothing, he affirmed that if the idea of perfection exists, there must necessarily be a perfect Being who created it—God.

In the following century, Isaac Newton (1643–1727), astronomer and mathematician, established the principles of classical mechanics in his treatise *Philosophiæ Naturalis Principia Mathematica (Mathematical Principles of Natural Phi-*

5 The term "scientist" was introduced in the 19th century. See Stanford Encyclopedia of Philosophy.

6 Three centuries later, Galileo, Spirit contributed to the codification of the Spiritism in chapter 6 (General Uranography) of the Genesis. (KARDEC, 1868)

losophy), written in Latin—the scholarly language of the time, also used by the Catholic Church, which then governed both science and society.

The *Principia* is a deductive work composed in the pure language of geometry. It revolutionized science and laid the foundations of modern physics and astronomy. Beyond its mathematical formulation of the laws of nature, the *Principia* presents a philosophical and scientific vision of the universe, discussing natural laws in a philosophical sense and exploring the nature of God's causal influence on creation.

In this remarkable work, Newton describes the atom as a divine creation and asserts that the Sun, the planets, and the comets could only be the work of an intelligent and powerful Being, whom he calls *Lord God Pantocrator*[7]—the Universal Sovereign:

> "This magnificent system of sun, planets, and comets could only proceed from the counsel and domain of an intelligent and powerful Being. And if the fixed stars are the centers of other similar systems, these, being formed by the same wise counsel, should all be subject to the dominion of Someone... This Being governs all things, not as the soul of the world, but as Lord of all; and because of his dominion he is usually called Lord God Pantokrátor, or Universal Sovereign"[8]. (Gasparini 2011, 1)

The Cartesian and mechanistic worldview dominated scientific thought—alongside the notion of a world governed by a controlling and dominating God—until the

7 Pantocrator means "Almighty" or omnipotence. The word derives from the Greek Pantokrator. The prefix "pan" means omnipotence and "kràtein" means power. The name Pantocrator also refers to the oldest icon of Jesus, found in the Saint Catherine's Monastery in Egypt.

8 Translated by the author, it was not directly excerpted from Principia, but the referenced article.

end of the nineteenth century. This anthropomorphic God imposed divine laws, accepted negotiations and offerings for the remission of "sins," and permitted the practice of external worship. The laws of classical mechanics proposed by Newton described the universe as a vast machine in motion. Since God ruled the cosmos, universal laws were seen as immutable and eternal—and, consequently, science regarded them as invariable as well.

The twentieth century, however, opened new horizons in the advancement of science. Field theory naturally evolved from the discoveries in electromagnetism—where light is understood as an electromagnetic field—initiated by Faraday (1791-1867) and Maxwell (1831-1879). This new perspective replaced the classical concept of force, which was associated with rigid bodies and characteristic of Newtonian mechanics.

Moreover, two groundbreaking theories reshaped modern science: Einstein's theory of relativity and quantum mechanics. As Planer observes in *Frontiers of Science*:

> "Einstein gazed at the macroscopic world and discovered the relativity of time and space and the relationship between mass and energy. Matter and energy are two different manifestations of the same physical reality. The world of energies is born, when condensed energy forms matter, i.e. matter is condensed light! Quantum mechanics explains the nature in its smallest, tiny part: the basic elements of matter, the subatomic particles, and everything that may have an equal or smaller size; therefore, it studies the behavior of matter and energy at the molecular, atomic, nuclear, and subatomic levels". (PLANER 2014, 8)

Although these theories expanded both scientific and philosophical perspectives, the Age of Enlightenment and the Industrial Revolution had already transformed society, reinforcing Descartes's legacy—the mind–matter dichotomy. This division led to the separation between the exact sciences and the humanities, as well as between science and religion. As a result, God and the soul (or Spirit) were gradually excluded from the scope of mainstream science.

In general, the traditional arguments of God's existence are ontological, cosmological, teleological,[9] and moral. According to Planer:

> "In the ontological argument, God is the essence of perfection; Its attributes are perfect, and It exists. The cosmological argument is based on the fact that God is the absolute and first Cause of everything. The teleological argument is based on the premise that only a perfect and harmonious Cause can give rise to the perfect cosmic harmony and the structure and order of the Universe. From the latter, it also derives the moral argument, in which the Creator in Its infinite existence and superb wisdom establishes the moral Laws". (Planer 2015, 8)

Several geniuses' philosophers or scientists support one or the other of these arguments of the existence of God, including Descartes, Newton, and the Dutch philosopher Spinoza (1632-1677), while others refute them. Another example is the German philosopher Emmanuel Kant[10] (1724-1804) considered the father of modern philosophy. Kant not only denies any theoretical argument of God's existence but also seriously criticizes any manifestation of external rituals, superstitions, and hierarchical order in the Church, which he sees as ways of trying to please God and thus

9 Ontology is part of the metaphysics (or philosophy) that studies the nature of being. Cosmology studies the origin, structure, and evolution of the universe. Teleology is the philosophical 'study of ends or purposes', i.e. it looks at the purpose of something by analyzing its results.

10 See also Kant's Philosophy of Religion in the Stanford Encyclopedia of Philosophy. Accessed on: https://plato.stanford.edu/entries/kant-religion/#KantCritTradArguForGodsExis, 28.07.2020

manipulating order to the detriment of moral principles.[11] In Kant's metaphysics, the existence of God, as well as the immortality of the soul and free will can only be accepted with rational faith.

Some scientists openly identify as atheists and deny the existence of God. Others remain comfortable with Descartes's dualistic view, in which God belongs to the domain of religion; thus, they set aside their personal beliefs when operating within the scientific environment. Yet there are those who acknowledge the grandeur of Divinity, perceiving God as inseparable from the physical universe. It is generally among this latter group that cosmological and even teleological arguments for the existence of God have emerged.

Contemporary Science and God

Science is produced by individuals—scientists and researchers—who are influenced by their religious beliefs, culture, and the society in which they live and move. Shaped by these influences, they construct their personalities and worldviews. Consequently, some may refuse to consider interpretations of scientific theories that transcend the realm of physical, material reality, as such interpretations may conflict with their personal convictions. Yet there are others who dare to look beyond, adopting positions that challenge the status quo and expressing their own vision of the world and of God.

In 1926, the American rabbi Herbert S. Goldstein asked Albert Einstein about his concept of God, after Cardinal O'Connor of the Catholic Church in Boston warned that the theory of relativity was "camouflaging atheism." Einstein responded by telegram, declaring:

11 See also Planer, Rejane. O Ponto Ômega. Presença Espírita.

> "I believe in Spinoza's God, who reveals himself in the lawful harmony of the world, not in a God who concerns himself with the fate and the doings of mankind."

Einstein rejected the anthropomorphic notion of God, which had given rise to a religion of fear. For him, the Jewish scriptures "illustrate the development from a religion of fear to a moral religion, which is continued in the New Testament" (Einstein, 1956, p. 27), and this moral dimension can also be found in Eastern traditions. However, Einstein identified a third stage of religious experience, which he called cosmic religion, in which there is no anthropomorphic conception of God.

> "The individual feels the nothingness of human desires and aims at the sublimity and marvelous order which reveal themselves both in nature and in the world of thought. He looks upon individual existence as a sort of prison and wants to experience the universe as a single significant whole." (Einstein 1956, 28)

Einstein stressed the difficulty of communicating to others this deep religious feeling that can be associated neither with a precise definition of God nor with theology because God is something that cannot be comprehended. For Einstein, this "cosmic religious feeling is the strongest and noblest incitement to scientific research" (Einstein 2006, 30), which he recognized in scientists such as Kepler and Newton, but also Democritus, Spinoza and Francis of Assisi. The spiritual mentor Joanna de Ângelis also says that this is the feeling of those who transcending the Ego, achieve full identification with the inner Self, and achieve the cosmic consciousness. (Franco 1993)

The interpretation of quantum mechanics has also been the subject of discussion since its early days. Quantum mechanics allows phenomena that are difficult to accept by more rigid minds linked to the mechanistic view of the world, which is the material and tangible reality that everyone experiences. For decades, most scientists have been satisfied with the minimalist and orthodox Copenhagen's[12] interpretation which left ontological questions aside.

On the contrary, Erwin Schrödinger (1887-1961) developed a fundamental part of this theory and also devoted himself to the analysis of the philosophical, ethical, and religious aspects of science. Schrödinger shared with Einstein the disdain for the orthodox interpretation of quantum mechanics, which implies the acceptance that, intrinsically, the laws governing matter are random. The famous theoretical experiment 'Schrödinger's cat' seeks to show the incongruity of this aspect of quantum mechanics. For Schrödinger, nature, human being, and God are perfectly integrated. Some interpret that in his way of thinking there was no room for God. However, Schrödinger did not affirm that but influenced by Eastern philosophical thinking, he built on the conception of the cosmological and omnipresent God, where everything exists and is connected to.

Despite the taboo of talking about God in the scientific environment, many renowned scientists have positioned themselves on the existence of God, and others have even proposed theories that include God as the primary and unique Cause, thus contributing to cosmological and teleological arguments about the Creator. Still, it seems odd to analyze God from the perspective of a scientific theory.

12 The **Copenhagen interpretation**, proposed by **Niels Bohr (1885–1962)**, holds that: there is no microscopic reality in itself—that is, there is no independently existing quantum world; events are observed through a process of wave function collapse, which occurs due to a probabilistic or non-deterministic process, such that when an event is observed, one of the many possible probabilities is immediately selected and the situation becomes concrete (wave collapse). Since physics is the result of measurements, there is no science beyond what can be measured.

Could the same science that emphasizes the material and tangible world and finds no room for the intelligent being - the Spirit - unravel the mystery of what God is? Certainly not. Astronomers and physicists argue, without an answer, about what there was before the creation of the Universe and what happened in the first moments of the *Big Bang*[13]. Science, in particular the cosmology, must face the mysteries of Creation.

In recent years, several hypotheses and theories have emerged that open the way for new scientific perspectives—ones in which Spirit (the individual and intelligent consciousness) and God are taken into consideration. Among these, we have selected two proposals from well-known mainstream scientists that include cosmological and teleological arguments for the existence of God. While some may dismiss these ideas as pseudo-science, others acknowledge the scientific foundation underlying their hypotheses and hope that future evidence will validate them.

In 1994, Frank Tipler, mathematician, physicist, and professor at Tulane University in the United States, developed the Theory of the Omega Point. This theory offers a new perspective on the creation and evolution of the universe by integrating science and spirituality through mathematical and physical principles. In his book *The Physics of Christianity* (Tipler, 2007), he emphasizes the necessity of accepting the implications of natural laws, declaring that:

> "If they lead to the proof of the existence of God, then we must accept that God exists."

As Planer observes, Tipler's theory is founded on three propositions:

"(1) life does not necessarily need to exist in the Uni-

13 Cosmology accepts that the Universe was created from a state of extremely high temperature and density and expanded to cooler state. See: https://wmap.gsfc.nasa.gov/universe/bb_theory.html

verse, but once it is, it can no longer disappear, but prevail in the Universe; (2) the Universe is expanding from the Big Bang until a moment of final contraction, where the great collapse of matter occurs; and (3) the available energy in the Universe is unlimited, which leads to the conclusion that the Universe does not end in a final state of maximum entropy, but in a state of eternal existence, or maximum storage and processing of information.

Tipler called omega point this final state of the Universe, which is not an "endpoint" of the Universe, but the extreme concentration of information, which would enable the re-creation of life or the Universe as a whole, i.e. the omega point would be a cosmological singularity". (Planer 2015, 9)

For Tipler, the cosmological singularity would correspond to the God of Judaism and Christianity. From the standpoint of Spiritism, however, the spirit is an individuality—a divine spark—created by God and destined to evolve continuously until attaining full knowledge of the divine laws. God, the Creator of all beings and all things, cannot be limited to a single point of singularity.

Some of Tipler's initial premises, first published in 1994, require reconsideration in light of subsequent scientific discoveries. For instance, the energy of the Higgs boson, detected in 2012, differs from the value assumed by Tipler. His theory also rests on hypotheses that still demand experimental verification and adjustment. Nevertheless, Tipler deserves credit for having built a bridge between science and spirituality, opening a path for others to follow.

In *The God Theory* (2009), Bernard Haisch proposes—drawing on the most recent developments in physics—that everything in the universe originates in God, the Supreme Intelligence or Consciousness, including matter, energy, and the very laws of nature in this and any other universe that may exist. For Haisch, God is the supreme and infinite Intelligence that creates the laws of the universe with the purpose of transforming potential into experience. The universe, encompassing all that exists, participates in its own creation, and "this ongoing, participatory act of creation is, in fact, the ultimate expression of God's love" (Haisch 2006, p. 44).

Haisch's cosmological and teleological argument is not intended to conceptualize God through scientific theory, as Tipler's does, but rather to guide science toward the discovery of God—to unite science and Divinity.

We are reminded of Kardec's words in *Genesis*:

> "In the state of inferiority in which humanity still finds itself, men can hardly understand that God is infinite." (Kardec, 1868 [1995], p. 61)

Certainly, we can intuitively perceive the Creator through creation, but to comprehend God fully remains beyond our current evolutionary stage. We can, however, feel the Divine Presence everywhere and marvel at the laws of nature; and through science, we may glimpse the immeasurable potential contained within Creation.

Even so, we must cultivate both reason and the strength of will to internalize a conscious and active faith. With clear and reasoned faith, we perceive God's presence in everything and everyone—from the smallest particle to the zygote that initiates life, and to the stars scattered throughout the cosmos. Such active and rational faith becomes unwavering, for as Kardec wrote:

> "Unshakeable faith is only that which can meet reason face to face in every human epoch." (Kardec, 1864 [1987], p. 203)

My faith may differ from yours. Each of us carries a personal heritage of knowledge, emotions, and experiences accumulated over many lifetimes. Yet, my God and your God are one and the same—the Creator of this magnificent universe filled with stars, planets, and all that we see and sense: a universe of light, for matter is intrinsically energy in vibration, and energy is ultimately light. When that light is divine and fecund, it manifests as Love, the source of all that exists, for the Apostle John affirmed: *"God is Love."*

And because God is Love, we have received the gift of life and the sacred opportunity to honor life in every form in which it manifests. Thus, we may worship God "in spirit and in truth," in accordance with the teachings of Jesus. The spiritual benefactor Joanna de Ângelis reminds us of our commitment to God and to Life when she emphasizes that we are heirs of God.

> "As a child of God, you are also a legitimate heir of the sublime ideals which will help you to expand your spaces, to understand the mechanisms of life, and to solve its challenging enigmas. You must be receptive to divine thought which permeates everything and everybody, so that you may also absorb it and put it into action." (Franco 1986, 32)

Bibliography

Capra, Fritjof. (1975, 1983). *The Tao of Physics.* Published, 1975; Publisher, Shambhala Publications.

Calovi, Gustavo Ellwanger. "A Questão de Deus no Contexto da Filosofia Moral de Kant." *Princípios - Revista de Filosofia,* Natal, v. 23, May-Aug 2016, pp. 171–191.

Einstein, Albert. (1956, 1984). *The World as I See It.* New York: Citadel Press Books.

Franco, Divaldo (spirit Joanna de Ângelis). (1982). *Spiritist Studies.* Brasília: Federação Espírita Brasileira.

Franco, Divaldo (spirit Joanna de Ângelis). (1993). *The Conscious Being.* Salvador: Leal Publisher

Franco, Divaldo (spirit Joanna de Ângelis). (1986). *Child of God.* Salvador: Leal Publisher

Gasparini, Eraldo Luis Pagani. (2011). "The Divorce Between Science and Religion." *Revista Brasileira de História das Religiões,* Maringá (PR), v. III, n. 9, Jan/2011. Available at: http://www.dhi.uem.br/gtreligiao/pub.html.

Haisch, Bernard. (2009). *The God Theory.* San Francisco: Red Wheel/Weiser.

Janiak, Andrew. "Newton's Philosophy." *The Stanford Encyclopedia of Philosophy* (Winter 2019 Edition), Edward N. Zalta (ed.). Available at:

https://plato.stanford.edu/archives/win2019/entries/newton-philosophy/.

Kardec, Allan. (1857, 1996). *The Spirits' Book.* USSF/ISC (2005)

Kardec, Allan. (1868, 2003). *Genesis: The Miracles and the Predictions According to Spiritism.* USSF/ISC (2005)

Kardec, Allan. (1864, 1987). *The Gospel According to Spiritism.* USSF/ISC (2005)

Moore, Walter J. (1989, 1998). *Schrödinger: Life and Thought.* New York: Cambridge University Press, pp. 172–173. Kindle E-book.

Pasternack, Lawrence and Courtney Fugate. "Kant's Philosophy of Religion." *The Stanford Encyclopedia of Philosophy* (Spring 2020 Edition), Edward N. Zalta (ed.). Available at: https://plato.stanford.edu/archives/spr2020/entries/kant-religion/.

"Kant's Philosophy of Religion." (2016). Accessed July 28, 2020, from https://plato.stanford.edu/entries/kant-religion/#KantCritTradArguForGodsExis.

Planer, Rejane. (2014). "Frontiers of Science: The Encounter Between Physics and Spiritism." *Presença Espírita,* 305: 8–13.

Planer, Rejane. (2015). "The Omega Point." *Presença Espírita,* 308: 8–10.

Tipler, Frank J. (2007). *The Physics of Christianity.* New York: Doubleday. Kindle E-book.

Suely Caldas Schubert was born into a Spiritist family; her paternal and maternal grandparents were Spiritists. She is a medium, lecturer, and author. She has four children, six grandchildren, and two great-grandchildren.

SCIENCE OF THE INFINITE

SUELY CALDAS SCHUBERT

Science of the Infinite! What an admirable expression from Allan Kardec—one that has captivated me ever since I first encountered it, long ago.

While reading the *Introduction* of *The Spirits' Book* (Kardec 2006, p. 51), I discovered that such a Science exists. It was an almost magical moment, for I immediately thought: *How marvelous!* There is an infinite science that embraces everything, that expands and reaches as far as our thought can go.

Countless ideas have occurred to me since then. I love reflecting upon the Infinite, attempting to glimpse something whose boundlessness fills me with wonder. In many of the poems I write, this theme appears again and again.

Naturally, the first and most immediate idea that arises in our mind is that which leads us to the Creator—to God—as Father, as the "Supreme Intelligence," in the sublime definition found in *The Spirits' Book*.

What interests us here, of course, is the context in which this subject is mentioned, as found in item XIII of the *Introduction* to *The Spirits' Book*, where Kardec refers to certain disagreements on important matters that were found among communications from Spirits regarded as superior—something that, according to some readers at the time, should not have occurred. Observe his words:

"We will say, first of all, that, apart from the cause we have just indicated, there are others capable of exerting some influence upon the nature of the answers, regardless of the Spirits' probity.

This is a crucial point, which can only be clarified through study. Hence, we say that these studies require prolonged attention, profound observation, and above all—as is demanded by all human sciences—continuity and perseverance. It takes years to become even a mediocre physician, and three-quarters of a lifetime to become a sage."

"How, then, can one hope to acquire the Science of the Infinite in just a few hours?" ***(emphasis added)***

Let no one be deceived: the study of Spiritism is vast; it encompasses all matters of metaphysics and social order—it is a world that opens before us. Is it any wonder, then, that mastering it requires time, much time indeed?" (Kardec 2006, p. 51)

Before us lies the Science of the Infinite, with all its infinite beauty, inviting us to know it.

Yet there is something very interesting to clarify: was this expression created by the Codifier himself? Let us analyze question 466 and its answer.

"Why does God allow Spirits to incite us to evil?"

Imperfect Spirits are instruments suited to test the faith and constancy of human beings in the practice of good.

As a Spirit yourself, you must progress in the Science of the Infinite. Hence, you must undergo the trials of evil in order to reach goodness. Our mission is to guide you along the right path.

Whenever evil influences act upon you, it is because you attract them through the desire for evil, for inferior

Spirits hasten to assist you in wrongdoing as soon as you wish to commit it. (...) Yet others will also surround you, striving to influence you toward good, thus restoring the balance of the scales and leaving you free to choose your actions. In this way, God entrusts to our conscience the choice of the path we should follow and the freedom to yield to one or another of the opposing influences that affect us." *(emphasis added)* (Kardec 2006, p. 51*)*

The answer, in its entirety, is quite clear, requiring no further commentary at this point. Yet, let us observe that the Spirit of Truth addresses the reader directly and firmly declares:

"As a Spirit, you must progress in the Science of the Infinite."

Thus, Kardec, grasping the significance of this statement, included it in the *Introduction* to the foundational work of Spiritism.

Infinite—an idea that leads us to God. In *The Spirits' Book,* Kardec and the Spirits of the Spirit of Truth's phalanx often refer to this essential quality of the Creator. For instance, in question 6:

"Could we say that God is the Infinite?"

Answer: "An incomplete definition. It reflects the poverty of human language, which is insufficient to define what lies beyond human expression." *(*Kardec 2006, p. 71*)*

And in question 13, the Codifier discusses the attributes of God:

"When we say that God is eternal, infinite, immutable, immaterial, unique, all-powerful, supremely just, and good, do we have a complete idea of His attributes?"

Answer: "From your point of view, yes, because you believe you encompass everything. Know, however, that there are things that surpass the intelligence of even the most enlightened human being—things your language, limited to your ideas and sensations, cannot express. Reason, in truth, tells you that God must possess these perfections in their highest degree, for if even one were lacking or not infinite, God would not be superior to all and, consequently, would not be God." (Kardec 2006, p. 75)

In *Genesis*, Chapter II, "The Divine Nature," Allan Kardec states:

> "God is infinitely perfect. It is impossible to conceive of God without the infinitude of perfections; otherwise, He would not be God, since one could always conceive of a being possessing what He lacked. That no being may surpass Him, it is necessary that He be infinite in all things." (Kardec 2002, p. 58)

Léon Denis affirms in *The Great Enigma* that God is "the Infinite Power that governs the world. Humanity is finite, yet it carries within itself the intuition of the infinite." (Denis 1983, p. 41)

At another point, he expands his reflection toward broader and infinitely eternal horizons:

"(...) Everything is linked and interconnected in the Universe. (...)"

Everything is summed up in a single, primordial power—the eternal and universal motor—known by many names, yet it is nothing other than Divine Thought, Divine Will. Its vibrations animate the infinite! All beings, all worlds, are immersed in the ocean of irradiations that emanate from the inexhaustible source. (Denis 1983, p. 41)

Spiritism opens limitless perspectives. The fascination awakened by these expansions of the soul stirs an indescribable joy, for, little by little, we discover that God is within us. This realization is profoundly irresistible—moving and eternal.

Thus, as we sense new possibilities for growth—not merely intellectual, nor confined to the speculations or musings of our consciousness, but something higher that begins to ferment within and pours forth into daily practice—we acquire precious and lasting treasures that transform our lives in their deepest and most definitive aspects.

Awakening to the reality of the Divine Presence in our lives leads us to an incredibly beautiful and transcendent certainty—one that expresses the impact of a love never before imagined.

Emmanuel, in one of his remarkable messages, granted me an invaluable expansion of thought—a discovery that arrived unannounced.

In the late 1990s, while reading *Living Spring*, chapter 30, something extraordinary occurred. It was not my first reading; Emmanuel's collection of Gospel commentaries had long been my parents' favorite choice to harmonize our home, and we were well acquainted with it. Yet one can read a page once—or many times—without perceiving its deeper meaning, which only reveals itself as the reader matures. It was then that I experienced one of those moments of insight.

Many know this passage, which I summarize here:

EDUCATE

"Do you not know that you are the temple of God, and that the Spirit of God dwells in you?" — *Paul (First Epistle to the Corinthians, 3:16)*

Within the tiny seed resides the germ of the beneficent tree.
In the heart of the earth dwell the melodies of the spring.

In the block of stone lie masterpieces of sculpture.

Yet, the orchard requires active labor.

The crystalline stream needs aqueducts to flow untainted.
The jewel of sculpture demands the miracles of the chisel.

"The Spirit also carries within itself the gene of Divinity. God is within us, just as we are within God." *(emphasis added)* (Xavier 2007, p. 77)

Highlighting:
"The Spirit carries within itself the gene of Divinity. God is within us, just as we are within God."

Discovering our divine genetics is simply astonishing! Understanding it in this way calls us to a series of new perspectives regarding infinite life—and the infinity within ourselves. We are children of God, and feeling this truth fills our souls completely.

Jesus often said "my Father":

"The works that I do in my Father's name, they bear witness of me." (John 10:25)

I have always found this statement of the Master gloriously beautiful and moving; yet we too can express ourselves in the same way.

The benefactress Joanna de Ângelis, corroborating this truth, adds:

> "All beings are of divine essence, for they proceed from the Creative Psyche, which establishes the process of evolution through the infinite experiences of unceasing progress." (Franco 2000, p. 111)

Spiritism is the Science of the Infinite that lifts the veil of the ages, allowing us, even now, to feel what Léon Denis already knew and longed to teach us:

> "Everything that is within us is in the Universe, and everything that is in the Universe is within us." *(*Denis 2010, p. 171*)*

We are citizens of the Universe—a realization of majestic and sublime magnitude.

Kardec, in *The Gospel According to Spiritism*, Chapter II, item 7, "My Kingdom Is Not of This World," expounds, with uncommon wisdom, the grand perspective that encompasses the trajectory of the Spirit, highlighting the solidarity that reigns throughout universal life:

> "Spiritism broadens thought and opens new horizons before it. Instead of the narrow and petty view that concentrates all attention on the present life, making the brief moment we spend on Earth the fragile pivot of eternal destiny, Spiritism shows that this life is but one link in the harmonious and magnificent chain of the Creator's work. It reveals the solidarity that unites all the existences of the same being, all beings of the same world, and the beings of all worlds. (...) This solidarity among the parts of one same whole explains what would otherwise appear inexplicable when seen from a limited perspective. Such understanding could not be grasped in Christ's time, which is why He reserved its revelation for future generations." *(*Kardec 2004, p. 79*)*

The idea of universal solidarity shines as an immeasurable expression of the Justice and Love with which God, the Supreme Creator, sustains the infinite vastness of His cosmic dwelling.

To conclude, let us listen once more to the voice of Léon Denis, who conveys to us, with infinite tenderness, some aspects of the Science of the Infinite:

"Little by little, the soul rises, and as it ascends, it accumulates an ever-growing sum of knowledge and virtue; it feels more closely connected to its fellow beings and communes more intimately with its social and planetary environment. (...)

Will the soul ever reach the end of its journey? Advancing along the path laid before it, it continually sees new fields of study and discovery unfold. It comes to perceive the sacred harmony of all things, to understand that there exists no discord, no contradiction in the Universe—that everywhere order, wisdom, and providence reign—and its trust and enthusiasm grow ever stronger. From that point onward, it becomes intimately united with the divine work, ready to fulfill the missions that belong to the higher souls, to the hierarchy of Spirits who, in various ways, govern and animate the Cosmos. These souls are God's agents in the eternal work of Creation; they are the marvelous books in which He has written His most beautiful mysteries; they are like currents that carry through the expanses of space the forces and radiations of the Infinite Soul." *(*Denis 2010, pp. 162, 172*)*

(May 30, 2020, Juiz de Fora - MG. BR)

Bibliography

The Jerusalem Bible. 2015. Published by Doubleday in the United States in 1966.

Denis, Léon. *The Great Enigma.* USSF

Denis, Léon. *Life and Destiny.* USSF

Franco, Divaldo P. (*Joanna de Ângelis, Spirit*). *Jesus and the Gospel in the Light of Deep Psychology.* Salvador: LEAL Publisher

Kardec, Allan. *The Gospel According to Spiritism.* USSF/ISC

Kardec, Allan. *Genesis.* USSF/ISC

Kardec, Allan. *The Spirits' Book.* USSF/ISC

Xavier, Francisco C. (*Emmanuel, Spirit*). *Living Spring.* FEB Publisher

Aluízio Elias Contributor to *Grupo Espírita Eurípedes Barsanulfo* [Euripedes Barsanulfo Spiritist Group], city of Uberaba, MG, Brazil.

THE WORD THAT CREATES

ALUÍZIO FERREIRA ELIAS

I - Prolegomena

Words attempt to express the Inexpressible—and yet, they define it. They whisper, delicately, how human beings experience their Creator. The heart beats, the soul radiates, and then words flow from their lips—an explosion of ideas. Drawings are etched on stone, then on ceramics and leather. Later, ink is impressed upon papyrus, parchment, and finally, paper.

A sharp question—bold, imprecise, eternal—arises: the question that touches the essence of all mystery... and it finds it, it reveals it: "What is God?"

God lives up to the deepest expectations. The Divine Being longs to reveal Itself—speaking through the sounds of Creation, sometimes whispered, sometimes thunderous... yet always audible. Thus, Its existence is as recognizable as the rivers and the birds.

But—*shh!*—we must be silent.

A profound stillness is needed to hear It—to hear God's love voicing kindness throughout our lives... this eternal Troubadour repeating Its ancient refrain: "I Am... I Am... I Am..."

And this is what Galileo declared, through the pen of Flammarion:

> "To those who already believe in the great voice of nature, I will say: Children of the new covenant, it is the voice of the Creator and the Preserver of beings, who speaks in the turmoil of the waves, in the sound of thunder; it is the voice of God that speaks in the breath of the winds. Friends, listen again, listen often, listen for a long time, listen always, and the Lord will receive you with open arms. O you who have already heard His powerful voice on Earth, you will understand it more fully in the other world."[14]

Thus, little by little, what had once been mere wind, breath, or voice—vowels, consonants, and digraphs—was transmuted into straight or slanted lines. God began to take the form of letters, a face within syllables; Its body became the Word. God was now read and reflected upon. Astronaut scribes arrived, exiled from distant constellations, and authored the undefinable divine semiosis—the sacred transmission of meaning. A collective legacy of spiritual expatriates endowed with a remarkable sense of divine enterprise, their audacity respectfully described by Emmanuel:

> "Since there was no writing in those remote times, all religious traditions were transmitted orally from generation to generation. However, with the assistance of exiled Spirits from the Capella system, the rudiments of the graphic arts received their first impulses, and a new age of spiritual understanding began to blossom in the realm of religious concepts."[15]

14 Allan Kardec. *The Spiritist Review - Journal of Psychological Studies*: October 1863. Trans. by the United States Spiritist Federation - Luiz A.V. Cheim.

15 Francisco C. Xavier, from the Spirit Emmanuel. *On the Way to the Light*. Trans. by Darrel Kimble, Marcia Saiz and Ily Reis. Brasilia: International Spiritist Council, 2011, p. 81.

The Hebrews did it with great mastery. Nomads, they spoke *of* God—and *with* God.

Even in captivity, they freed their tradition from the limitations of oral recitation and chose to preserve their sacred legacy in writing. For centuries thereafter, they continued to record their reflections on Yahweh—a mixture of insight and Revelation.

It was the vocation of that people—liturgical and theological in nature. An articulate nation, they earned this observation from Emmanuel:

> "The books of the Israelite prophets are filled with enigmatic and symbolic words, forming a partially deciphered monument to the secret knowledge of the Hebrews. Yet, despite their mysterious character, taken as a whole they compose a poem of eternal clarity. Their songs of love and hope have crossed the ages with the same indestructible flavor of faith and beauty. That is why, like the Gospel, the Old Testament is touched with immortal light, illuminating the spiritual vision of every heart."[16]

The Hebrew language was the first to provide accounts of the Infinite; or, at least, the most consistent ones. And it spoke of an unlimited God - so immense that the Universe is contained within It. And it did this by making use of a monosyllable. Even before the unpronounceable four consonants of the mystical Tetragram, God is simply El (אל). The marriage between an Alef (א) and a Lamed (ל) forged the most elementary notion of God's importance.

16 Xavier, *On the Way to the Light,* p. 67.

II – The Driving Force

We're all on our way. Our feet trample the dust of the stars, leaving traces in time. The starting point is the Creation; the end is perfection. On this journey, each individual only has their own actions and the succession of existences. What moves us? What kind of engine draws us? Why can't we remain motionless, whereas moving seems to be an irresistible force?

The answer is God. God is the lever that moves everything. For this reason, when they name It *El (אל)*, Abraham's descendants ended up adding a unique concept (essential attribute of the Most High). It's that, in proto-Hebrew, the *Alef (א)* had a pictorial form (prior to its modern schematic expression). Since it was the first letter of the Hebrew alphabet, the one that goes ahead of them all, it made allusion to bovine work as a draft animal; to the energy of cattle (used for moving heavy loads), and from this idea we have its most representative spelling: the head of an ox 𐤀.

For the Ancient Hebrews, God was force in the form of movement. The most powerful impulse of all Nature, setting everything into perpetual motion. Stars orbit in the center of systems and galaxies, while those circulate throughout space. The light of the Supernova continues to travel, even after the star is dead. The Sun and the Moon agitate the waters of the ocean. The Earth spins, enabling the alternation between day and night, light and darkness. The unforgettable teacher of Lyon, contemplating this vital dance, commented:

> "Plants are born, grow, thrive and multiply always in the same manner, each one in its species, by virtue of these same laws. Each progeny is similar to the one from which it came out; growth, flowering, fruit bearing, and coloring are subordinated to material causes, such as heat, electricity, light, humidity, etc.

The same is true of animals. The stars are formed by molecular attraction and move perpetually in their orbits by the effect of gravitation. This mechanical regularity in the employment of natural forces does not denote the activity of free intelligence. [...] The useful suitability of these forces is an intelligent effect that denotes an intelligent cause. A pendulum moves with automatic regularity, and its merit lies in this regularity which renders it useful. The force which activates it is entirely material and not at all intelligent; but what would this pendulum be if an intelligence had not combined, calculated and distributed the use of this force to make it function with precision? [...] The same applies to the mechanism of the universe, God does not show Itself, but attests Itself through Its works."[17]

Beyond the corporal mobility of humans, there's a kind of movement that isn't taken into account very often. The Being, not the body, is the one who moves uninterruptedly. We are Spirits on a journey through space and time. We are born, we grow and we die; and after that, we are reborn. We often switch roles between wise and fool, patrician and plebeian, everywhere, breaking boundaries, inhabiting many different bodies. Reincarnation, under the strategy of the Divine intelligence, places us in different cultures and different roles within the same families.

And the will of God knows how to use individual discomfort for the collective good. Being the Lord of Life, It decides when and where a person will be born and die. It may place Bedouins in the tropics, and Aimores in the desert; peasants in castles and nobles in huts, coercing change every time that free will subverts the idea of freedom. God

17 Allan Kardec. *Genesis - Miracles and Predictions According to Spiritism.* Trans. by the United States Spiritist Federation (H.M. Monteiro), 2020, Part 1, Ch. II, It. 6.

uses the strong arm of Its will, so that the sharpness of the circumstances will reinforce the Law, forcing humans to move, until they ask "where to?"

And the Most High responds with love. God is guidance, always showing the right direction and correcting our course. Then there is the qualitative presence of the letter Lamed (ל) in the word El (לא). The proto-Hebrew designates that its iconography indicates the subsistence of the tribes of Palestinian pastors. Lamed (ל), at first, was a shepherd's staff . Shepherds were zealous for their sheep and goats. Their staff was their guiding instrument and they guided their flock, offering them direction and protection.

That's how God acts in our lives. The Creator encourages movement, provides direction, shows the path and establishes the goal to be reached. The Divine Being corrects our mistakes and puts us back on track, always protecting us. Emmanuel, in this regard, comments:

"Observe God's protection that surrounds your steps at all times, especially when inhibition and exhaustion draw near. [...] Divine Providence grants you means, above your strength, to cooperate in the edification of the common good, of your own free will, without being compelled by the circumstances. In other words, God helps you to help yourself, and the Creator will always provide you with the utmost assistance, as long as you play your part in the development and improvement of the Work of the Creation, doing the bare minimum of what you are able, what you know and what you must do."[18]

God, called El (לא) by the Hebrews, is the directional dynamo. Since we remain under safekeeping and are pro-

18 Francisco C. Xavier, from the Spirit Emmanuel. *Segue-me!...* [Follow Me] 10th ed. Matão: O Clarim, 1996, p.183-184.

tected at all times, we ask our readers: "Who will stay inert?!" We always move according to a gentle flow, or something like that, blown away by harsh winds that take us where we should go. This is the first idea, the foundation of all deep spirituality in the world. God: The Force that drives us.

III - The Strength of the House

The essence of each being is an area still under construction, yet to be completed. God is a fabulous architect who standardized the foundations of Life. The Eternal Genius delineated a general outline for all humans, but, at the same time, It has established a specific project for me as the writer and another for you as the reader. However, filling the gaps within our souls with *thinking* and *thinkable matters,* as well as building our own edification, are our individual tasks. In the course of our lives, an abstract manufacturing process takes place, a labor for our inner benefit, using ethereal masonry.

Critical moments and complications arise when our egotistical whim, as servant-builders, clashes with the project of the Architect-Engineer. The layout sets the direction, but the free will of the builder leads somewhere else. Many mistakes are committed during the execution of the project: walls fall, columns crumble, ceilings collapse, floors crack...

This is when the building becomes vulnerable. And at this moment of great danger the Lord of the factories visits the ruined construction site to comfort the builders, encouraging them and pointing out the necessary repairs. Purpose is restored, morale is boosted and the original project is resumed. At each new enterprise, an operational tool is added. Everything becomes more sophisticated and complete (less tent, more mansion; less beast, more human).

Instructor Calderaro made an accurate comment on this subject:

> "We are not miraculous creations destined as adornments of a cardboard paradise. We are God's children and heirs, acquiring qualities from experience to experience down through the millennia. There is no favoritism in the Universal Temple of the Eternal, and all the powers of the Creation are perfected throughout the Infinite: the embryonic consciousness existing in the rock that rolls along with the river current is involved in a process of emergence. The trees, often standing tall for hundreds of years, enduring the gales of winter and lulled by the breezes of spring, are developing memory. The tigress licking her newborn offspring is learning the rudiments of love. The ape, through its shrieks, is developing the faculty of speech. Yes, God has created the world, but we are still far from the completed opus, as the beings that inhabit the Universe will toil in sweat for a long time improving it. The same goes for us individually. We are the Divine Author's creation and we must perfect ourselves completely. The Eternal Father has established as a universal law that perfection must be a work of cooperation between Him and us, His children."[19]

When the creation becomes humanized, each one of us shares their habitation with God; they cohabit the core of each person's mind. Since God is Omnipresent, the Creator is certainly also within us. Henceforth, let us try to understand how this coexistence takes place: the creation bumping into the Creator at all times, switching between impulses and thoughts.

19 Francisco C. Xavier, from the Spirit Andre Luiz. *In the Greater World.* Trans. by Darrel W. Kimble and Ily Reis. Brasilia: International Spiritist Council: 2010, p.44.

Jesus was the one to shed more light on this issue. He captured the attention of humans regarding this divine assistance when he referred to God as "Our Father". That is because the evolving mind has the characteristics of a house or a dwelling place. It starts as a tent or a cabin and as it improves, it reaches the level of a mansion or small palace. We live within ourselves, thus. God is "Our Father", to whom that unforgettable psalm proclaimed by Christ is addressed. Av (בא) is the word that opens the prayer poem and can be translated as *dad* or *daddy*. Let us make note of the affectionate tone expressed by this Hebrew word. An Alef (א) and a Beit (ב) meet for the formation of a significant monument.

The Alef (א), as we have seen, is the strength. The Beit (ב), in its proto-Hebrew roots, used to be represented pictographically as the interior of a house, a dwelling place. Thus, we inevitably consider that this Av (בא), or "Our father", according to Jesus, is the Strength (א) of the House (ב). And since each being lives within oneself, because our minds are our permanent residence, we conclude that God, being the Av (בא) of all humankind is the sturdy support of all mental houses in the process of improvement.

As a protector of our habitation, God upholds our essence, keeping our home standing. It proposes the use of good judgement, temperance and balance between reason and emotion. It strokes our forehead, embraces us, nourishes us, wraps our hearts. Without God the house would be prone to demolition. Without this Father, our Av (בא), humans would fall, torpid and fatigued.

That is why Calderaro made use of this metaphor (house) to describe the psychic structure of Spirits:

"We cannot say that we have three brains simultaneously. We have only one, which is nevertheless divided into three distinctive regions. We could picture it as a three-story castle: on the first floor, we find the 'residence of our automatic impulses', symbolizing the living summary of the work we have accomplished. On the second, we find the 'domicile of current acquisitions', where the noble qualities we are building are developed and consolidated. On the third, we have the 'home of superior concepts', indicating the higher qualities we must yet attain. In the first, dwell habit and automatism; in the next, effort and will; in the last, the ideals and higher goals to be reached. In this way we distribute the subconscious, the conscious and the superconscious among the three stories. As we can see, we possess within us the past, the present and the future."[20]

God, the daddy who sustains the residence, is located by Calderaro on the third floor, where the 'ideals and higher goals' vibrate... at the summit, the top... in the sky of the house. Jesus placed God in space when he recited: "Our Father who art in Heaven"; would that have been fortuitous? Certainly not. God extends Its regenerative power down to the lower floors, pouring out blessings from top to bottom. But that happens only when humans (the individuals who, together, build and inhabit their houses with God) evoke It in the Heights; if people go up to the third floor and return from there with the Laws in their arms, to restore order or regain strength, like a Moses on behalf of themselves.

IV - Conclusion

We recognize God is much more than these verbs we use to define It. The Divine Being is more than the moving, driving and supporting force. God possess virtues we still do not know and is also everything that our phonetics and semantics cannot yet reach; the indescribable and unpronounceable; sounds and letters we cannot fathom, in-

20 Xavier, *In the Greater World,* Trans. by Darrel W. Kimble and Ily Reis. Brasilia: International Spiritist Council, p. 46.

scribing the divine characters within the gaps of the hidden cosmos.

But these things we have considered – two words and four ancient letters - award the human spirit with unparalleled comfort. Knowing that God is our Driving Force and the Strength that support our mental house is reason enough to provide us joy and security. Knowing that the Creator drives and guides us, that the Lord builds and sustains us helps us to sense some happiness. It feels good to think that we will never be inert and lost; that God will always be around, every step of our way, offering guidance; that we will not collapse, broken into ruins.

All of this because God is the Lord of Abraham, the Father of Jesus, and is with us in our thoughts during our journey; whether spoken or written, coming out of the mouths of everyday people or from the scrolls of the wise; when we cry "My God! My God!" seeking help, in our daily lives, or seen as the Supreme Intelligence, the first cause of all things, as described in Allan Kardec's first book.

The one who, sovereignly, is.

Décio Iandoli Jr. holds a doctorate in medicine from Universidade Federal Paulista (UNIFESP). President of the Medical-Spiritist Association of Mato Grosso do Sul and Vice-president of the International Medical-Spiritist Association.

WHAT IS GOD?

DÉCIO IANDOLI JR.

For us, inhabitants of this beautiful little blue planet, engaged in the adventure of discovering cosmic and spiritual consciousness, everything seems to require a definition; everything must be explained and understood—like curious children who ask their parents countless times a day: *Why? Why? Why? Why?*

However, to define is to set a limit, to establish a boundary, a beginning and an end to something. Here we already encounter the first of many challenges we face when we seek to "know" or discuss God: how can we define what has never begun, what has always existed? How can we define what never ends, what is infinite? What has no limits? As Isaac-Félix Suarès[21] said, "Any definition is a limit"[22].

I overcome this first obstacle by proposing not a *definition* (which becomes impossible along this line of reasoning—at least in our limited understanding), but by replacing it with another concept: a *characterization* or *conception*. I must confess that this latter term pleases me greatly, for to have a *conception* of God is to give birth to or create within ourselves an idea or thought that characterizes God—something that allows us to perceive the Divine through our childlike minds, to sense what God represents, even without being able to fully comprehend God.

21 French poet and writer (1868-1948).

22 See https://dicocitations.lemonde.fr/citations/citation-15676.php [consulted 20.10.2020]

That said, I propose a search for a *concept* of God—a concept that may shape within us the idea of God. To this end, I turn to the book that brought the Spiritist Doctrine to light: *The Spirits' Book*. In it, Allan Kardec, in "Book One," Chapter One—entitled "God"—asks the very first question (Kardec 2020, p. 39):

"What is God?"

We can observe that Kardec was careful not to ask *"who"* or *"whom,"* but rather *"what."* This is an important detail—overlooked in some Portuguese editions of the book—since it avoids presupposing or framing the question in a way that might suggest a preconceived answer. This choice demonstrates not only Kardec's seriousness and discernment but also his profound wisdom. After all, the premise he followed was that God could neither be a *someone* nor merely a *something*.

The answer that follows is:

> "God is the Supreme Intelligence, the First Cause of all things."

Supreme Intelligence. First Cause. There we have it: a magnificent concept—far deeper and more complex than it may seem at first glance.

Supreme Intelligence is the intelligence above all intelligences. *First Cause* refers to that which precedes all known and unknown causes; that which has always existed, the source and origin of everything and everyone.

If God is neither someone nor something, if God is the cause of all that exists, then God cannot be contained within the limits of our intelligence—as the Brazilian philosopher Huberto Rohden insightfully observed when he asked:

> "Human being! You, who do not understand the artifact—do you intend to understand the artificer?

> What kind of God would that be, one that could fit within your intelligence? A sea that could fit into a seashell—would it still be the sea? A universe confined within a thimble—what name would it deserve? The infinite circumscribed by the finite—would it still be infinite?" (Rohden 1998, p. 25)

We encounter something remarkable here, for the doctrine codified by Allan Kardec in 1857 offered humanity a rational path toward understanding and accepting God – even amid the profound ignorance in which we still find ourselves – and challenged us to grasp something that transcends one of our deepest and most fundamental references: time.

For us, everything must have a "before" and an "after." Everything must have a beginning. Even when we are capable of accepting something without an end – the infinite – it remains extraordinarily difficult to conceive of something without a beginning. How, then, can we comprehend that which has always been?

I admit that it is difficult to free ourselves from the concept of time. Yet I have reason to believe that time, as we perceive it, does not truly exist. Time would be an illusion produced by the contact of our consciousness with deeper reality – a perception that helps us interpret what surrounds us in a logical manner, but which is not an objective reality. It is a subjective experience, a byproduct of our interaction with the environment. It is, however, far from meaningless, for we truly need this notion of time in order to evolve and to relate to reality.

Nevertheless, in the search for God – the origin of all that exists – illusion serves us little. God transcends this image we call "reality," which Plato so aptly described in the *Allegory of the Cave* as mere shadows of what *is*, rather than *what is in itself*.

Even if this line of reasoning may seem to drift in a whirlpool of inconsistent ideas, the initial difficulties yield a pearl – something precious for us, incarnate beings living on a planet of atonement. They provide the perception of a concept that grants logic and meaning to existence – not only our own existence but the existence of everything – since every intelligent effect requires an intelligent cause.

Otherwise, we would have to admit that "nothing" could give rise to "something," and such reasoning seems not only inconsistent but also irrational and illogical. For "nothing" is that which does not exist, and what does not exist cannot create or originate anything. For those who seek truth and use science as a means to reach it, it is essential to uphold logic and reason.

Given the complexity and perfection we observe in life and the cosmos – with all their astonishing and precise natural laws – we must ask: What is their cause? If the beginning of the universe is explained by a great explosion, who caused the explosion? What exploded?

Something must have caused the Big Bang – what was it? And if we were to discover the cause of the beginning of the universe, another question would inevitably arise: What caused that cause? And so on, until we reach the *First Cause*, a *Supreme Intelligence* capable of creating all that exists – God.

As André Luiz reminds us:

> "Human intelligence understood the greatness of the Universe and perceived its own humility, recognizing within itself the inalienable idea of God." (Xavier 1997, p. 151)

Change the name if you will, alter the perspective, but we will always face the need to acknowledge a *First Cause* — not through faith alone, but through logic: an intelligent cause behind all intelligent effects that surround us, in countless forms and on countless levels.

It was this God that Kardec presented through the fundamental and brilliant question that opens his work:

"What is God?"

Three simple words that hold within them the power to awaken in us the very conception of the Creator.

This God, the *Supreme Intelligence,* lifts us beyond the limited and impoverished view of an anthropomorphic deity who, even today—and still among us Spiritists—lingers in our minds, giving us the impression that God is like us: capable of punishing, taking revenge, granting privilege, or destroying. These traits belong not to divine nature but to our own moral primitiveness.

Father Hipólito reminds us in *Workers of Eternal Life*:

> "In truth, the anthropomorphic religions of the Earth's crust have poisoned our minds, instilling false conceptions of God into our reasoning." (Xavier 1998, p. 126)

The concept of God offered by the Spirits is the *real* God — the God of science, philosophy, and, ideally, of religion as well. It is the God of logic and reason, inviting us to move beyond rigid definitions and to find meaning in what we cannot yet comprehend. This understanding serves as a starting point for a new discovery of ourselves and of the greater reality in which we are immersed, though we rarely perceive it.

The reflections presented above might seem to distance us from God, suggesting a condition of inescapable automatism from which there is no escape. Yet, although we may feel distant from God, God is ever near to us, for we are the *creatures*, and God is the *Creator*. Our ignorance does not separate God from us – it only prevents us from perceiving God most of the time.

Nonetheless, it becomes essential to free ourselves from the anthropomorphic image of God and to embrace the responsibility entrusted to us along with our free will. We are not *things*; we are *beings* – created and perfectible intelligences in evolution. To accept our responsibility means ceasing to attribute our triumphs and failures to external forces, even to an anthropomorphic God who is not even a shadow of what *Supreme Intelligence* truly signifies.

> "As for the rest, it is essential to recognize that the debtor is bound to the commitment assumed. God created free will; we created fatality. It is therefore necessary to break the handcuffs we have placed upon ourselves." (Xavier 2008, p. 307)

We are neither abandoned nor lost. There is order and law guiding us toward perfection. Yet we also possess freedom of choice and the capacity to learn – and this must propel us forward. We originate from the Creator, and our evolution will ultimately lead us back to the Creator, even though God has always been here with us, while we are still absent from God.[23]

23 I remembered the story of the *footprints in the sand*, which tells that, at the end of a journey along the beach, a man—walking absentmindedly—suddenly perceives the presence of the Father beside him. Looking back, he notices two sets of footprints imprinted in the sand along the entire path, except at the most difficult and dangerous points of the way.
Perplexed, the man asks:
– Lord, I know I didn't even notice Your presence, but why, precisely during the most dangerous and painful moments, were You not by my side?
The Lord then asks gently:
– Why do you think I wasn't with you?

"Evolution is our slow journey back to God." (Xavier 1995, 179)

Thus, everything that is, that exists, comes from God and exists in God:

> "It is up to us, therefore, to note that the cosmic fluid or divine plasma is the force in which we all live, in the varied angles of nature, which is why it has already been stated, and quite rightly, that "in God we move and exist."[24] (Xavier 1997, 25)

Admitting all our limitations, which is already a sign of learning[25], we are able to perceive from nature, which is nothing more than the set of divine laws, the concept of God as essential for the advancement of our pretensions to know the universe and its laws. It also helps us to understand who we are, where we came from and where we are going, issues as old as our own existence, because God is container and content, God is all and God is a fraction, God is everything. The only "uncreated" that exists is God, since God created everything and, therefore, what God did not create, does not exist, cannot be considered.

> "God is not the God of the dead, but the Father of creatures that live forever." (Xavier 2013, 293)

God is just, for justice is immutable perfection. Being perfect, God has no need to evolve; yet, God is dynamic, for perfection itself moves—unceasingly creating more perfection, radiating what is perfect as It has always done. Not

---

The man replies:
– Because in those parts of the path, there is only one set of footprints.
The Lord smiles and explains:
– Yes, those are My footprints. Because in your most difficult moments, I was carrying you in My arms.

24 Paul of Tarsus, Acts, chapter 17º, verse 28. (Note of the spiritual author).

25 For as Socrates said, "I only know that I know nothing".

"from the beginning," because for the Creator there was no beginning—only for that which was created.

We are creatures and co-creators, for free will grants us the power to create. We are perfect, as is all that God has made, though still incomplete, since we are in the process of formation. From all of creation, we receive the elements necessary for us, one day, to be able to understand and perceive God—or, as Jesus said, to be "face to face" with God—perceiving God within creation, while we still barely perceive ourselves.

This is because we carry within our essence the resemblance of the Creator, which is our intelligent nature. Yet what we create is not eternal, unlike what is created by God. André Luiz expresses this beautifully when referring to the created intelligences:

> "These Glorious Intelligences take the divine plasma and convert it into cosmic dwellings of multiple expressions—radiant or obscure, gaseous or solid—obeying predetermined laws, as abodes that last for millennia and millennia, but that wear out and transform, since the created spirit can form or co-create, but only God is the Creator of All Eternity." (Xavier 1997, p. 21)

Feeling God—who is so near to us, in all that surrounds us—is what remains to us, as it has always been. We are creatures who bear within ourselves the essence of the Creator. We are part of a Whole still unimaginable to us, yet real—far more real than our material experience can reveal, far truer than the "truths" we believe we know.

It is therefore the destiny of science—which seeks truth—to one day know God, for truth and God are one and the same.

Bibliography

KARDEC, Allan. 2001. *The Spirits' Book*. [Translation by USSF].

ROHDEN, Humberto. 1998. *From Alma to Alma*. São Paulo: Editora Martin Claret.

XAVIER, Francisco C. (André Luiz, Spirit. 1997. *Evolution in Two Worlds*. FEB Publisher.

XAVIER, Francisco C. (André Luiz, Spirit). 2013. *The Messengers*. FEB Publisher.

XAVIER, Francisco C. (André Luiz, Spirit). 2008. *Nosso Lar*. FEB Publisher.

XAVIER, Francisco C. (André Luiz, Spirit). 1998. *Workers of the Eternal Life*. FEB Publisher.

XAVIER, Francisco C. (André Luiz, Spirit). 1995. *And life goes on*. FEB Publisher.

Humberto Schubert Coelho Spiritist worker at *Sociedade Espírita Primavera.* humberto-schubert@yahoo.com.br

THE CONCEPT OF GOD

HUMBERTO SCHUBERT COELHO

Before being distorted by cultural relativism, Philosophy was primarily characterized by meditation on the highest form of thought—the contemplation of the ultimate causes of all things and natural laws. The idea of the "highest thinkable thing" was defined by Aristotle as Theology, the science of God. Thus ended the Classical period of philosophy—represented by Socrates, Plato, and Aristotle—whose central thesis affirmed that one absolute and intelligent cause forms the foundation of all beings.

Hellenistic philosophy, which dominated Western culture from the empire of Alexander the Great through the first centuries of Rome, recognized its inability to elevate the human spirit to the same divine heights reached by classical thought. Consequently, it turned toward the world in search of solutions to the enduring problem of human happiness, yet repeatedly returned to the concept of God as the only possible basis for such a solution.

With the rise of Christianity, a new school of thought emerged—no longer speculative but transcendently inspired, grounded in experience and intimate familiarity with the Divine. Christianity softened hearts that had been impervious to intellectual appeals and introduced to humanity the notion of love—closely linked to a God of infinite paternal compassion and a personal commitment to the beings created by Divine Mercy. Humanity was thus revealed as children of God, in contrast to the earlier conception of an impersonal, almost logical God-force, or Logos, of the Greeks.

Western civilization later reaped the bitter fruits of its excesses and ambitions and fell into centuries of suffering. Yet, within the silence of souls, it matured the elevated concepts of old, witnessing a patient harmonization between Greek rationalism and Christian mysticism, which eventually produced Francis of Assisi and Thomas Aquinas as ultimate models of understanding Christianity—the first as a practical exemplar, the second as a theoretical architect.

The Reformation then arose as a spiritual and moral reaction to the many corruptions of the Church of Rome. Reformers strove to free Christianity from hollow rituals, moral decay, and the submission of Christ's Church to worldly influences. However, they failed to convert hearts to genuine Christian living, for their own hearts remained unconverted. In the end, they built churches much like those they had sought to reform or dismantle. Nevertheless, this anticlimax did not prevent the renewal movements of both the Renaissance and the Reformation from partially achieving their aims—establishing a freer and more plural understanding of life, the world, and the Sacred Scriptures, thereby giving rise to modern thought.

In the wake of this idea of individual freedom, countless missionaries carried these principles forward—sometimes in material progress, improving the conditions of life; at other times in spiritual and moral dimensions, in perfect harmony with the superlative wisdom of Socrates, Plato, and Jesus.

Developing the modern, subjectivist, and critical spirit, Descartes affirms in his *Principles of Philosophy* (1644):

> "The more we perceive something to be perfect, the more we must believe its causes to be perfect."[26]. In-

26 René Descartes. *Los princípios de la filosofía* [*The Principles of Philosophy*]. Barcelona: Alianza Editorial, 1995, 31.

deed, the causes of the soul must be something greater than the soul itself—more intelligent, freer, and morally superior—or else it could not have created it. It is irrational to claim that the human soul originated from nothing or from matter, both of which lack its attributes and perfections.

In the twentieth proposition, Descartes reinforces:

"We are not the cause of ourselves."

If we cannot fully comprehend ourselves or the things around us, or the manner in which our intellect grasps them, how could we possibly possess the idea of a supremely perfect Being above us, if not because that same Being has implanted within our souls these notions—the idea of God and of the Divine attributes—which shine within us, though they transcend our limited intellect?

It is for this reason that the idea of infinity, which exists within us—finite beings—both inspires and humbles us. (*Descartes, 1995*)

John Locke (1632–1704) classified divine revelation into two types: general (indirect) and special (direct)—the latter expressed through prophets or Christ—affirming that one could never contradict the other. He was followed by Isaac Newton, who likewise rejected the doctrine of the Trinity. Around the same period, Fénelon (1690–1710) refined Descartes' rationalist philosophy, offering a subtler proof of God's existence and demonstrating the impossibility of materialism.

Shortly afterward (1730–1750), Voltaire led a movement of consciousness in defense of freedom, opposing superstition and what he called the "laziness of reason." He promoted a secular understanding of God—not one who loves and reveals Himself only to Jews and Christians, but one present in the hearts of all peoples, the children of the Almighty.

Finally, Alexander Baumgarten (1714–1762) clarified the distinction between the concept of God revealed directly in the Bible and that revealed through reason, concluding that reason alone suffices to lead any rational being to glorify the Supreme Author of all things.

Humanity's spiritual restoration in the Modern Era begins with Gotthold Ephraim Lessing (1729–1781), who, in *The Education of the Human Race*, proposed the idea of progressive revelation—that truth unfolds through a process akin to scientific discovery. At no moment do we possess absolute truth, but rather a collection of studies, revelations, and reflections proportional to our spiritual capacity. When we are ready, God permits new direct revelations through prophets and mystics, or allows more mature souls to elaborate new insights by their own efforts.

Lessing concluded that such mature souls could not have been created innately superior to others; they must have begun as simple and ignorant as all spirits. The only rational explanation reconciling God's justice with the existence of spirits at different stages of development is the principle of reincarnation.

A disciple of Pestalozzi, Allan Kardec benefited from a bilingual (Franco-German) education that enabled him to study deeply the works of major French and German thinkers. Pestalozzi himself, an Enlightenment philosopher, regarded God as the causal principle of all things and refused to confine the Divine to the cultural traits attributed to God by Jews or early Christians.

From this Enlightenment tradition, Kardec learned that the Gospel must be read in the light of reason—and never the other way around. Truth must not be bent to accommodate the letter of Scripture, especially since, as Kardec observed, the Sacred Texts were written in symbolic and mystical language (*Kardec, 2005*), which prevents literal interpretation and demands a critical key for comprehension.

For both reason and the Bible, God stands as the central point around which all ideas and thoughts—past, present, and possible—gravitate. No idea can sustain itself when detached from a metaphysical foundation—a nexus of meaning that gives it coherence and justification.

Since the time of Socrates and Plato, it has been understood that materialistic philosophies, which deny God as the source of reality, inevitably collapse under the impossibility of justifying themselves as coherent systems of thought. The alternative to philosophy, which finds in God the mental foundation of all existence, is the self-contradictory doctrine that what is observed by the mind—matter—is the foundation of the mind itself. From this anti-philosophical notion emerged the later and equally inconsistent doctrines of psychoanalysis, Marxism, and positivism, all born in the 19th century during an age when cultural hostility toward religion refused to acknowledge that the metaphysical basis of human thought is the idea of God.

While acknowledging that such doctrines contributed intellectually to humanity's progress—despite their rejection of metaphysics and religion, and though partially justified by the failures of institutional Churches—it remains clear that restoring a rational worldview requires dismissing any system that seeks to escape the idealistic foundation of reality.

One of the greatest merits of Spiritism is that it aligns itself with this long tradition of idealism, rationalism, and theism—the very essence of philosophy and human thought—at a time when such ideas were in decline, eclipsed by their opposites.

It is both beautiful and meaningful that Kardec begins and ends the principles of Spiritist philosophy—*The*

Spirits' Book and *Genesis*, respectively—by studying the concept of God, as if to remind us that no subject holds greater sovereignty than the Author of the cosmos.

"The most important part of Christ's revelation—in the sense that it is the primary source, the cornerstone of His entire doctrine—is the entirely new point of view by which He portrays the Divinity."[27] (Kardec 2011). This passage carries several philosophical dimensions. It presents Jesus as a philosopher; it demonstrates Kardec's deeply philosophical concern with the primary cause underlying all phenomena and things; it points to the method and perspective through which one should begin to interpret the moral laws and facts within the Gospels; and it encourages meditation on the concept of God as a path toward resolving other fundamental philosophical questions. These dimensions, as can be seen, operate simultaneously on theoretical and practical levels.

As an Enlightenment thinker, Kardec conceived the idea of God with a grandeur that rises above narrow religious and human interests—above the notion of a limited or anthropomorphic God. As a Spiritist, he made it clear that it is Jesus' superior philosophical insight that sustains both the faith and the moral depth of His doctrine—an achievement that would be impossible without an equally elevated foundation.

Free from dogmatism, Kardec, in his rational compilation of the teachings of the Spirits, does not offer a stagnant or fixed concept of God. Like Immanuel Kant, the great philosopher of the preceding century, Kardec organized questions and answers in a way that reveals the conjectural nature of the concept of God. Spiritism, therefore, does not impose a ready-made or immutable idea of the Divine upon its followers; rather, it of-

27 Allan Kardec. *Genesis: miracles and predictions according to Spiritism.* Trans. USSF - 1st ed, 2020.

fers a horizon through which reason perceives the highest summit of its present understanding of truth.

In the first chapter of *The Spirits' Book*, human reason—represented by Allan Kardec—addresses itself and Heaven in inquiry about the infinite and supreme intelligence that would be the cause of all things. The responses received are not idols to be worshipped or frozen into certainties, but rather guidelines for reflection and progress.

Later, when outlining the moral laws, Kardec and his spiritual interlocutors adopt the same approach. Instead of establishing rigid codes of external behavior, they emphasize abstract principles that empower individuals to discern, through reason and conscience, the most dignified, peaceful, and constructive path toward happiness.

By purifying religion through the sound filter of reason and controlled experimentation, Kardec bestowed upon humankind an exalted vision of the miraculous source of being—so lofty that, when we begin to grasp it, our souls fall into reverent silence and radiant adoration.

Bibliography

DESCARTES, René. *Los princípios de la filosofía* [The Principles of Philosophy]. Barcelona: Alianza Editorial, 1995.

KARDEC, Allan. *Genesis: miracles and predictions according to Spiritism*. Translated by USSF 2020.

——— *The Gospel According to Spiritism*. Translated by USSF 2020.

——— *The Spirits' Book*. Published by USSF/ISC 2025.

Eulália Bueno Lar Espírita Caminho do Cristo, Santos, SP - Brasil.

THE EVIDENTLY INVISIBLE

EULÁLIA BUENO

A Legend of Unknown Origin titled "Signs of God" tells us that an illiterate old Arab used to pray every night with such fervor and devotion that one day, the wealthy leader of a caravan called him over and asked:

– Why do you pray with such faith? How can you be so sure that God exists if you cannot even read?

The humble believer replied:

– Great lord, I know that our Heavenly Father exists by the signs that He leaves.

– What do you mean by that? – asked the chief, intrigued.

The servant explained:

– When you receive a letter from someone, how do you recognize who wrote it?
– By the handwriting.

– And when you admire a piece of jewelry, how do you learn who made it?
– By the goldsmith's mark, of course!

– And when you hear the footsteps of animals around your tent, how do you know whether it was a sheep, a horse, a camel, or an ox?

– By their tracks!

The old believer smiled and continued:

– Then come outside the tent, my lord.

He pointed toward the sky, where the moon shone surrounded by a multitude of stars, and said reverently:

– My lord, those signs up there could not have been made by human beings!

In that instant, the proud caravan leader surrendered to the evidence. There, in the sand under the silvery light of the moon, he knelt and began to pray.

As the great French poet Victor Hugo once said:

"God is the invisible made evident." (Buchbaum 2004, p. 288)

Our mind, still so limited, feels humbled before the Divine Work. Yet at the same time, it marvels at its beauty and rejoices in being part of Creation – and in having the ability to seek understanding of it.

Although modern science, through astrophysics and astronomy, continuously observes and discovers the formation of new stars, planetary systems, and stellar explosions within a universe full of activity – proving that only a Supreme Intelligence could create something so perfect – there are still those who do not believe in God.

Throughout history, in times of great suffering and turmoil, there have been movements denying the existence of God. One such moment took place in France, in November 1793, at Notre-Dame Cathedral in Paris, when Pierre Gaspard Chaumette, a revolutionary leader, proclaimed the death of God on French soil. He and his followers declared that France, having freed itself from the Bourbons without divine help — since God had not intervened to ease the people's suffering — had no further need of Him. This sparked a wave of similar proclamations, asserting that humanity had no need for spiritual reality, especially the Divine itself.

The institutional Church was stripped of its property; episcopal palaces were sold; and places of worship were closed or repurposed — such as La Madeleine Church, in Paris, transformed into a pantheon honoring Voltaire, Rousseau, Benjamin Franklin, and other luminaries and "martyrs of liberty."

The German philosopher Friedrich Nietzsche, in *Thus Spoke Zarathustra*, used the voice of the madman to ask poignantly:

> "If God is dead, who will light the stars at night?
>
> Who will feed the birds and the fish in the sea?
>
> If God is dead, what are cathedrals for? Are they mausoleums of the image of God?"[28]

Researchers claimed that the soul did not exist. They said: *We have dissected thousands of corpses and found no soul. The soul, they argued, was a product of the brain, just as bile is a product of the liver and urine of the kidneys.*

Thus, although the 19th century is regarded as the Century of Enlightenment, materialism dominated human thought.

Regarding this period, we must mention the beautiful message entitled "Kardec and Napoleon" (*Xavier, 1966*), which describes a sublime assembly that took place on December 31, 1799, when wise and benevolent Spirits gathered in the Higher Spheres to mark the beginning of the new century.

28 Cf. Lecture delivered by Divaldo Pereira Franco, titled *"Proofs of the Existence of God"*, held on March 4, 2017, at the Centro Cultural Cenecista Joubert de Carvalho, in Uberaba - MG.

Napoleon Bonaparte, then First Consul of France, disengaged from the body during sleep, also attended that meeting to reaffirm his redemptive commitment—one that would free him from the pride deeply ingrained since the times when he appeared on Earth as Caesar. Proud and unyielding, while others shed tears of deep emotion, he remained with dry eyes before the greetings of several Roman legions, symbols of the revival of power amid the challenges that inspired his mission in France, still distant from the greater purposes for which he had been destined.

It was the dawn of a century meant to be illuminated by the light of the Third Revelation, and Napoleon, once the great Caesar, assumed the responsibility of safeguarding the spiritual mission of the Disciple of Jesus. The message highlights:

> "Here gather with us laborers of all ages. Patriots of Rome and Gaul, generals and soldiers who followed you in the conflicts of Pharsalus, Thapsus, and Munda, remnants of the battles of Georgia and Alesia—here they meet you with sympathy and expectation...
>
> In the past, enthroned in absolute power, you claimed descent from the gods to dominate Earth and annihilate enemies.
>
> Now, however, the Supreme Lord has granted you as cradle an island lost in the sea, that you may not forget human smallness, and has determined that you return to the heart of the people whom you once humiliated and mocked, so that you may secure for them their immense mission before Humanity in the century we are about to begin.
>
> Placed by Divine Wisdom as helmsman of order amid the sea of blood of the Revolution, do not forget the mandate for which you were chosen." (Xavier 1966, p. 125)

The message highlights precisely the period of the French Revolution, when the great Apostle of Jesus returned to Earth under the name Hippolyte Léon Denizard Rivail, on October 3, 1804, exactly two months before Napoleon Bonaparte's coronation as Emperor of France, in a grand ceremony held in the same Cathedral of Notre Dame where God had once been denied.

After signing a concordat with the Vatican through a decree, Napoleon Bonaparte brought God back to France, leading many of his former opponents to surrender to faith, declaring themselves returned to the Divine embrace—humbled, repentant, and sorrowful. Once again, God triumphed over the arrogance of human ignorance.

Thus, to the sound of music composed for the occasion—"Pomp and Circumstance"—sung by a choir of two hundred voices, the Pope entered the splendid nave of the Cathedral carrying the crowns on a richly adorned cushion, only to be surprised by Napoleon's audacity, who took the crown and crowned himself Emperor of France, later crowning Empress Josephine, a clear demonstration that, in that country, even religion—or God—would be subject to his authority.

This was the same Napoleon who once questioned the French astronomer and physicist Pierre-Simon Laplace (1749–1827) about his book *The Celestial Mechanics* (1796), asserting that he found no reference to God within it. Laplace replied with the sarcasm of one who believed to have all answers regarding Creation:

"I had no need of that hypothesis, sir."

Napoleon recognized the Roman Catholic Church but refused to submit to it. His coronation took place in the Pope's presence but lacked any sacred character. Civil marriage and divorce were maintained, and in 1804, he instituted a Civil Code devoid of any religious reference.

In this distance from God, humanity itself became responsible for repairing social injustices and inequalities—issues that could not be better understood precisely because of the denial of the soul and the Divinity.

This movement continued to advance because, unfortunately, the mark of modernity also represents the rise of atheism among arrogant and prideful individuals, driven by purely material interests—such as the philosopher Karl Marx (1818–1883), one of the most radical followers of Hegel (the late philosophy professor at the University of Berlin). Marx asserted that true power did not reside in religion but rather in the material world, in the possession of property and capital. In the material world he envisioned, God disappeared. God became, as for Laplace, an unnecessary hypothesis. The phrase that summarized Marx's thought was:

"Religion is the opium of the people." (*Critique of Hegel's Philosophy of Right – 1844, Introduction*), concluding that religion was an alienated operation, an illusion, the inverted reflection of the real world.

With *On the Origin of Species by Means of Natural Selection,* published on November 24, 1859, Charles Darwin opposed the Christian version of the creation of the world and became one of the most contested scientists of his time. According to Darwin, we are nothing more than upright-walking mammals. The century's great shock was complete: humanity ceased to be in the image and likeness of God to become a descendant of the ape. At that time, Darwin did not have the courage to say this openly, although he certainly must have speculated about it.

Only two years after the publication of the masterful *The Spirits' Book* (1857), Allan Kardec opens it with question number 1 - *What is God?* The Codifier introduces a profound philosophical shift in the act of thinking about God: to think without modeling, without preconceived notions, freeing us to adopt a way of thinking detached from any image—whether consciously or unconsciously imagined. Kardec invites us to reformulate our understanding of God. When the answer speaks of a *Supreme Intelligence,* it leads us beyond material things, prompting us to seek something transcendent in relation to what affects our senses.

We perceive that we are not forced to accept the idea of God, but if God exists, then He can only be a *Supreme Intelligence* capable of creating all that the Universe contains, while God infinitely expands.

All the assertions made by philosophers and scientists of that era regarding the denial of God mainly revealed their total ignorance of the aforementioned work (*The Spirits' Book*), as they presented arguments grounded in logic for a possible refutation—but such refutation was never made. The same can be said for the conclusions of Jean-Martin Charcot[29] (1825-1893) who between 1880 and 1890, dissected thousands of brains in search of the original source of madness and other illnesses that affect human beings. Among other findings, his studies, conducted at the Salpêtrière University Hospital, concluded that hysteria was located in the brain and not in the uterus, and that the classic symptoms of this illness—as well as those of epileptics and neurasthenics—could find explanations and experiences rooted in the past, thereby giving rise to hypnosis. He also studied neurasthenics and epileptics, and his contributions became effective both in neurology and in psychology.

Charcot had a profound scientific spirit and, for this very reason, did not reject any possibility. It is regrettable that he did not study the works of Kardec, perhaps influenced by the prevailing mindset in French society, which—

29 Jean-Martin Charcot was a French physician and scientist who gained renown in the fields of psychiatry and neurology during the second half of the nineteenth century. He was one of France's greatest clinicians and professors of medicine and, together with Guillaume Duchenne, is considered the founder of modern neurology.

despite the advances offered by science—still clung to the prejudice that everything related to God belonged exclusively to the domain of religion.

The pseudonym Allan Kardec was not recognized by the French Academy of Sciences, and no one imagined that behind it was a highly respected disciple of Pestalozzi—Hippolyte Léon Denizard Rivail, an influential educator, author, and translator.

God is expressed in all the works of the Codification with judicious clarity. In the development of the questions that unfold masterfully in *The Spirits' Book*, the section dealing with the proofs of God's existence includes the beautiful question:

> "Where may we find proof of the existence of God? – In an axiom that you apply to your sciences: there is no effect without a cause. Seek the cause of all that is not the work of humankind, and reason will answer you. To believe in God, it is enough to cast one's eyes upon the works of Creation. The Universe exists; therefore, it has a cause. To doubt the existence of God would be to deny that every effect has a cause, and to affirm that nothing can produce something." (Kardec 2016, p. 54)

From here, reason calls us to pursue further reflections.

The Spirit is the Intelligent Principle of the Universe, created by God, and through its interaction with matter, it evolves by means of experience, acquiring memory and, with it, the knowledge of things—eventually becoming capable of making choices and reaching free will.

In the same book, we find two other questions that deserve the deep reflection of science:

"Is the spirit independent of matter, or is it merely

> a property of it, as colors are properties of light and sound is a property of air? - Both are distinct, but the union of spirit and matter is necessary to give intelligence to matter." (Kardec 2016, p. 61)

And further:

> "Then, are there two general elements in the Universe: matter and spirit? - Yes, and above all, God, the Creator, the Father of all things. These three elements constitute the principle of everything that exists—the universal trinity. But to the material element one must add the universal fluid, which plays the intermediary role between spirit and matter proper, which is too coarse for the spirit to act directly upon it." (Kardec 2016, p. 61)
>
> "... And while the boldest minds analyze the occurrence of the Big Bang—especially its first three minutes—not a few attempt to impose the idea of self-creation, dismissing the presence of God." (Franco 2010, p. 16)

Following, for a moment, the reasoning of scientists and philosophers who proclaim self-creation, we are still left to ask: from where did the material that originated the explosion come? How could disorder have produced the infinite stability and beauty of the Universe? How did this material differentiate itself into inorganic and organic matter? It becomes necessary to accept that where our intelligence cannot yet reach, there are still realities that demonstrate the presence of an uncreated antecedent—whatever name one chooses to give it.

Thus, we immerse ourselves in the knowledge of André Luiz, when he says:

> "The cosmic fluid is the divine plasma, the breath of the Creator, or the nervous force of the All-Wise.

> In this primordial element, constellations and suns, worlds and beings vibrate and live as fish in the ocean." (Xavier and Vieira 2015, p. 19)

We may then perceive that there is a generating source of life throughout the Universe, far beyond our comprehension, because even to manipulate such matter it is necessary to be able to perceive the Divine Will and to possess sufficient capacity to work with this primordial element. Who could be capable of carrying out such a task?

> "In this original substance, under the influence of the Supreme Lord, divine Intelligences joined to Him operate in an indescribable process of communion—the great devas of Hindu theology or the archangels of various religious traditions—drawing from this spiritual breath the storehouses of energy with which they construct the systems of immensity, in a co-creative service on a higher plane, in accordance with the designs of the All-Merciful, who makes them guiding agents of the sublime Creation." (Xavier and Vieira 2015, p. 19)

> "Faced with everything that impresses us—the variety and perfection that move us when we look upon Nature, whether purely material or animated—within all the calculations of probability that involve attempts and errors, it is impossible to accept that chance could create and succeed in processes as complex as life in all its intricacy. That would be to admit life as the result of mere luck or coincidence." (Nascimento 2015, p. 25)

> "The universal source of intelligence is God. And God creates both the material and the spiritual principles. These associate so that the spiritual principle may develop through the Law of Evolution, following the paths that life offers it—from the most rudi-

mentary bacteria, through humankind, and up to the state of Angelic or pure Spirit." (Nascimento 2015, p. 142)

"It is in those beings, which you are far from knowing completely, that the intelligent principle develops, individualizing itself little by little and preparing itself for life. It is, in a certain way, like germination, by which the intelligent principle undergoes a transformation and becomes Spirit. Then begins the period of humanization, with the awakening of self-awareness, the capacity to distinguish between good and evil, and the responsibility for one's actions (...)." (Kardec 2016, p. 277)

Deeply rooted in instinct, this "hidden force that drives living beings to perform spontaneous and involuntary acts for the sake of self-preservation. In instinctive acts, there is neither reflection nor premeditation." (Kardec 2013, p. 69)

It is interesting to observe that instinct, not possessing the nature of intelligent acts and lacking discernment or free choice, nevertheless never fails—it is always accurate and reliable! What lies behind the astonishing mechanism that makes a plant turn toward the sun, a flower open and close, and animals instinctively protect their offspring from danger—something that, many times, intelligence fails to accomplish?

We realize that instinct, wherever it manifests, acts precisely, forcefully, and successfully, without distinction among beings. Intelligence, however, demonstrates the existence of individuality, endowed with the ability to choose differently and which "reveals itself through voluntary, reflective, and premeditated acts, combined according to the opportunities of circumstances. It is, incontestably, an attribute exclusive to the soul." (Kardec 2013, p. 70)

It becomes very clear that all this represents the evolution of the Intelligent Principle through different stages. While it has not yet reached the age of reason and free will, "something" chooses on its behalf with such wisdom and precision as to protect it as a parent would a small child—guiding its steps safely until it reaches maturity, when it becomes responsible for its own decisions.

There remains one more question to ponder: if we evolve at different paces and instinct always acts in a flawless way, its control cannot belong to any individuality, since we do not find within incarnate or discarnate creatures the qualities necessary for such guidance. We must look much higher—to the Creator—and understand that all beings are immersed in the Universal Cosmic Fluid, or the mental breath of God, which at first acts uniformly and broadly upon all. When self-governance becomes possible, however, this Divine Action gradually yields space to the autonomy of intelligence and free will, allowing beings to grow and evolve, assimilating experience and knowledge until, from instinct, only the records of evolution remain and the Spirit attains the summits of possible perfection.

How can we deny the unique, absolute, and perfect action, if we do not accept an Intelligence that surpasses the greatness of creation and, in the name of science and precision, offer to nothingness—to chaos—the supreme condition of such order?

On the contrary, when we accept the logical deduction of this Supreme Intelligence, which creates simple and ignorant spirits, we begin to better understand all the interconnections of the Universe and of life, gaining a purpose for our own existence. We can then clearly situate ourselves within the evolutionary chain, recognizing our intellectual—and above all—moral smallness. We also begin to comprehend so many absurd reactions that have punctuated the history of humankind, not only in France, during the pre- and post-Revolution periods, but also throughout the ages, when the human creature—barely distinct from the anthropoid apes—manifested religiosity through bizarre acts and offerings, in keeping with mistaken beliefs, striving to please God by every possible means to attain desired ends. Today, we can no longer think that way.

Throughout the course of the ages, we should free ourselves from the chains of instinct and choose lucid reason—yet one that is humble, capable of lifting, along with intellectual progress, moral virtues. We must cease to view ourselves merely as material beings, prioritizing bodily needs to the detriment of spiritual values. We must acknowledge, without question, that a cell phone, a computer, an automobile, an airplane, and other technologies of our era require an intelligence capable of such elaborate creations. And yet, we look at the sky, at nature, at the cellular intimacy that sustains us, and we question whether these were or were not the result of the chance that supposedly began with the Big Bang!

Why deny the obvious? Only a Supreme Intelligence could surpass and explain all that exists.

How many times have we denied God precisely at the moment when the Divine manifestation is undeniable! How many times have we refused to see that the tragedies which afflict us are the result of our limited intelligence, imprisoned by purely material values that generate far more suffering than joy or happiness.

During the two great wars that shook the foundations of the Earth throughout the 20th century, widespread revolt once again brought the denial of God—as though God were responsible for the very freedom granted to us, for the infinite capacity to make choices, and even through the pain we choose to endure, to continue the infallible educational process of our souls.

It was in the first half of the 20th century that Dr. Abraham Cressy Morrison (December 6, 1864 - January 9, 1951), who served for 40 years as director of the Museum of Natural History and the Academy of Sciences of New York, examined that immense wave of materialism and wrote a text later transformed into the book *Seven Reasons Why a Scientist Believes in God*, published in January 1964.

Based on this text, the Bahian orator Divaldo Pereira Franco presents, in his lecture titled *"Proofs of the Existence of God"*, a profound reflection on faith, reason, and the harmony between science and spirituality."[30]:

> "Not believing in God, under the claim that science has not proven His existence, ends up being worse than believing in Him for scientific reasons."

I propose that we place ten coins, numbered from 1 to 10, inside a pocket and then shake them. Let us try, without looking, to draw them out in the same numerical order. Mathematically, the chance of picking number one correctly is one in ten; to pick numbers one and two in that sequence is one in one hundred; the chance of getting them all right, from 1 to 10 successively, is one in ten billion.

THEREFORE, I BELIEVE IN GOD—the One who created the conditions for our planet to exist. But I believe in God for a second reason, which is called life. If I were to ask each of you what life is, everyone would give a different definition—no two would be the same. A biologist would say that life is the result of cellular automatism, biological fatality; a philosopher would call it an enchanted journey through the land of fantasy; a poet, a writer, a farmer, an illiterate person—each would define life according to their own perspective. And yet, no one has ever managed to de-

30 Lecture delivered on March 4, 2017, at the Centro Cultural Cenecista Joubert de Carvalho, in the city of Uberaba, Minas Gerais - Watch on YouTube.

fine life in its entirety, because life eludes us—it is the result of the phenomenon of cellular division, which multiplies until life takes shape. But life is a wonderful chemical miracle; that is why I believe in God—because of the miracle of life.

I also believe in God for a third reason, which is called the instinct of animals. We all talk about instinct, but no one knows where it resides. We say, "I pulled my hand away by instinct," "I reacted by instinct." It's just a word, yet we still do not know how this mechanism works. We do not know, for example, why the salmon, when the spawning season arrives, leaves the rivers where it lives and swims against the current to spawn in the very place where it was born. If we catch a salmon and release it in a tributary of the same river, it realizes the mistake, holds back its spawning, and continues swimming until it finds the waters of its birthplace—and only then does it die. Who taught this to the salmon?

The wasp, when it is about to lay eggs, knows many things. It knows that insects are born adults and hungry, so it must provide for its offspring, which can only eat live flesh—if they eat dead flesh, they die. So, the wasp digs a hole in the ground, creates a small underground chamber, gathers some clay, and seals the entrance. Then it flies off to find a larva or a grasshopper, stings the grasshopper to paralyze it—no one has yet been able to inject the exact amount of venom needed to paralyze without killing. The wasp carries the grasshopper back to the burrow, lays its egg near the insect's abdomen, seals the hole, flies away, and dies. When the larvae hatch, they begin eating the grasshopper from the abdomen up to the head, and by the time the grasshopper dies, the young wasps are ready to fly and live independently. Who taught the wasp this process? If it erred, all wasps would perish.

When eels reproduce, all of them—throughout the world—leave the waters of rivers, seas, and oceans and swim toward the Sargasso Sea, the deepest region of the oceans. There, they reproduce and die, while their offspring return to the same waters from which their parents came. European eels, because they are farther away, delay their reproduction by a year to arrive at the same time as their American sisters. And never has an American eel been found in European waters, nor a European eel in American waters. Why?

I also believe in God for a fourth reason, which is called genes and chromosomes, for we are all the result of them. If we were to reduce the Earth's population—billions of people—to the scale of genes and chromosomes, all of humanity would fit into a thimble and still not fill it.

Thanks to these discoveries, I BELIEVE IN GOD! But I believe in God for a fifth reason, which is called intelligence, because instinct is like a monotonous note that always repeats itself. The first ovenbird acted this way, and the last will act the same—but intelligence is the capacity to conceive, to describe the entire symphony of nature—and that is why I believe in God.

I believe in God for a sixth reason: the balance that exists in the ecosystem. We know, and have already said, that every insect is born an adult. Insects breathe through tubes, and as they grow, the tubes do not; therefore, they die from lack of air. Science has already identified 750,000 families of insects on Earth. Imagine if they kept growing and their tubes grew as well! If that were the case, we could find ants the size of elephants and fleas as large as rhinoceroses—what would become of us then?

And I BELIEVE IN GOD for a seventh reason, which is called imagination. Only through imagination can one conceive the inconceivable; only through imagination can one think of the finite within the infinite. It is imagination that allows me to conceive of GOD, as the psalmist David said in Psalm 19:1: *"The heavens declare the glory of God, and the universe speaks of the work of His hands."*

Indeed! If, on a winter's night, under a clear sky without artificial light, we walk along a road and look up, we will be dazzled by the stars and exclaim, "My God, I see millions of stars!"—and yet we are mistaken, for only 5,000 stars are visible to the naked eye—actually 2,500, since the other 2,500 are on the opposite side of the planet. With binoculars, we could see 15,000; with a medium telescope, 150,000; with the Mount Palomar Telescope in California, 30 million; and through the Hubble Telescope, we could see a billion stars—only within our galaxy.

I BELIEVE IN GOD, and immediately we are moved by emotion. Before this infinite greatness, the English astrophysicist Dr. James Jeans said to us, who are not astronomers:

"If you wish to have an idea of the distances that separate the stars from one another, take a supersonic airplane, fly over Eurasia, take three bees, release them through the window, and they will have less space to fly than the stars have in infinity."

And we will begin to understand the grandeur of creation when we look at our Sun and realize that the heat we receive results from its internal combustion, as it burns 420 million tons of mass per second, converting it into energy. This means that in about 15 million years, the Sun will die—and with it, our entire solar system.

If we prick ourselves with a pin, we destroy thousands of capillaries—yet others immediately take their place. If we suffer a cut, bleeding begins, and what does the organism do? It condenses at the wound site a special substance, forming a clot that stops the bleeding—an immediate, intelligent response.

The individual places a hand upon their head and is holding the most remarkable computer humankind could ever imagine! Inside this skull, in the brain, there are one hundred billion neurons—nerve cells that never repeat. Once formed, they are responsible for our memory, express our intelligence, and are all interconnected through the so-called cerebral synapses.

Then, instinctively, we place a hand upon our chest—the heart, that marvelous pump, the most resilient organ known to humankind. Nowhere on Earth exists an elastic mechanism like it. It begins to beat after conception, and when it stops, biological life ceases. This heart is so extraordinary that it pumps blood at a speed of 70 meters per second, singing the glories of God.

Faced with so many wonders, we are compelled to bow down and say: I BELIEVE in God!

But God is far more fascinating—for as Saint John the Evangelist declared: "God is love."

God will remain in the infinity of space and in the vastness of the cosmos, and also within our very being.

To find God, it is not necessary to travel outward, but inward—tuning in to the divine vibration that is, in truth, the essence of ourselves—and to finally say:

> "No, my God, I do not merely BELIEVE in You. I am CERTAIN of Your existence!"

Bibliography

BUCHBAUM, Paulo. *Frases Geniais que Você Gostaria de Ter Dito.* Rio de Janeiro: Ediouro Publicações, 2004.

FRANCO, Divaldo P. (*Joanna de Ângelis*, Spirit). *Entrega-te a Deus.* Catanduva: Intervidas, 2010.

KARDEC, Allan. *Genesis.* USSF 2020.

KARDEC, Allan. *The Spirits' Book.* USSF 2020.

NASCIMENTO, Otacino R. *Das Causas Primárias, De Deus.* Goiânia: FEEGO, 2015.

XAVIER, Francisco C. (*Irmão X*, Spirit). *Cartas e Crônicas.* Brasília: FEB, 1966.

XAVIER, Francisco C.; VIEIRA, Waldo. (*André Luiz*, Spirit). *Evolution in two worlds. FEB Publisher*

Arismar Léon Radiologist, coordinator of the study of André Luiz's works and facilitator of the study of *The Mediums' Book* at the Brazilian Spiritist Federation; president of the Spiritist Medical Association of the Planalto (AME-Planalto) and collaborator of the Family Department of the Spiritist Medical Association of Brazil (AME-Brazil).

BEYOND MATTER: SCIENCE, SPIRITISM, AND THE EXPANSION OF THE NATURAL WORLD

ARISMAR LÉON A. PEREIRA

"What is essential is invisible to the eyes."
— Saint-Exupéry

The relationship of human beings with their environment involves a mixture of curiosity, fascination, and awe in the face of the vastness and power of the unknown. We admire what we most fear, and we fear what we most admire. In this ambivalent relationship, we seek to understand what surrounds us, who we are, and where we come from. Religion, science, and philosophy are complementary paths we follow in this search.

At first glance, religion and science — two great systems of human thought — may seem discordant, incongruent, or irreconcilable in their approaches. However, upon deeper analysis, we are led to see that they are intricately united by the same premise: that we live in a universe whose origin lies in a remote past. Philosophy presents us with the problem of the "first cause." How did the universe begin?

For many religions, this universe originated from the intentionality of an intelligence, a super-consciousness, Divinity, or God. For science, this element may be represented by a set of circumstances or conditions, not necessarily intentional or self-aware.

Yet a central question must be considered in this search, within all paths of human thought: can we truly comprehend the first cause, our reality, and all that surrounds us through our consciousness and senses — even when amplified by the instruments we have created?

The spiritual benefactors tell us that this is not possible, for we lack the sense (Kardec 2013, 57) that comes from the complete purification of the Spirit (Kardec 2013, 51). Can we measure infinity with a ruler?

Like fish in an aquarium, we are aware of greater realities beyond our confines, but we cannot comprehend them, for the essential escapes our eyes. Science and faith are, in a sense, like windows that open onto the invisible and the unknown, guiding us beyond the limited capacity of our sensory perception.

At this point, we enter a crucial field that often causes disagreement in the dialogue between faith and science. This invisible world that is presented to us — does it belong to the natural or the supernatural world? Since it is the role of science to study the natural world, there seems to be no space in it for the supernatural or the miraculous. And it is precisely here — unlike what we see in other religious traditions — that a bridge arises between Spiritism and science. For both, the invisible world is part of the natural world and extends it. It is substantial and material, though made of a kind of matter that, in most conditions, escapes both our senses and instruments.

> Kardec beautifully presents this expanded vision of reality when he says: "Expelled from the domain of materiality by science, the marvelous took refuge in spirituality, where it found its last stronghold. By demonstrating that the spiritual element is one of the living forces of nature, a force that incessantly acts in concert with the material force, Spiritism restores to the realm of natural effects those that had been removed from it, for such effects, like others, are subject to laws. If it were expelled even from spirituality, the marvelous would no longer have reason to exist, and only then could it be said that the age of miracles has passed." (Kardec 2013, p. 232)

By demystifying the marvelous, Spiritism places the spiritual world within the reach of scientific study and progress. Through scientific investigation, the invisible becomes more accessible, allowing humanity to explore the unknown and expand the boundaries of the natural world. In some instances, this expansion is profound and transformative, deepening our understanding of the essential laws of nature – and, consequently, bringing us closer to Creation and to God.

For example, in 1610, with the publication of *Sidereus Nuncius* by Galileo Galilei (1564–1642), humanity transcended the frontiers of a geocentric worldview to embrace a heliocentric one – vast and immeasurable, with its diverse nebulae. Later, in 1687, Newton (1643–1727) published his *Mathematical Principles of Natural Philosophy,* expanding our understanding of the natural world through his new mathematics and gravitational law. Then came Darwin (1809–1882), in 1859, with *On the Origin of Species,* demonstrating natural selection and the progress of species in the material realm. And finally, Einstein (1879–1955), with his *General Theory of Relativity* published in 1916, revolutionized our understanding of the universe and its laws.

As significant as these milestones were in expanding our view of the natural world, we must also highlight the experimental and systematic work conducted by Professor Hippolyte Léon Denizard Rivail, in April 1857, with the publication of *The Spirits' Book*. From that moment onward, an immeasurable expansion of the natural world and its laws began.

The metaphysical realm – previously constrained by dogmatic interpretations, personal conjectures, and fantasies, and relegated to the supernatural – became tangible, "palpable," and substantiated. It revealed its own laws, operating in harmony with natural laws, including moral laws that govern our relations with the visible world. These immutable laws resonate with the teachings of the great spiritual masters of humanity, converging toward the lessons of Jesus.

In this way, Spiritism broadens the field of scientific study, as Kardec affirms:

> "Materialism can thus see that Spiritism, far from fearing the discoveries and positivism of Science, goes toward them and even provokes them, for it possesses the certainty that the spiritual principle, which has an independent existence, cannot in any way be harmed by them." (Kardec 2013, p. 180)

Interestingly, by adhering to the postulates of logical positivism – limiting itself to the study of matter, its composition, interaction, and transformation, that which can be verified, measured, and observed – science has encountered a paradox: it moves from the measurable material world into the domain of the unknown and "immaterial" aspects of the universe.

This movement began in the 17th century, with Galileo Galilei's establishment of modern experimental science and continued through Newton's laws of gravitation, leading to a mechanical and predictable view of nature. The universe was conceived as a gigantic machine, built upon absolute structures of space and time, where every event was a calculable consequence of a prior cause – the doctrine of determinism.

However, this mechanistic and deterministic vision began to shift in the 18th century. For philosopher and mathematician Leibniz (1646–1716), the concept of "force" underwent a radical transformation – from a mechanical principle to one of vital activity. Force was intrinsic to matter, representing its deepest nature. It was not something that acted upon a body but rather something the body inherently possessed – the *vis viva* ("living force").

This concept later proved crucial in studies of temperature and heat. The research of physician Julius Mayer (1812–1878) led to the concept of energy – a manifestation of this living force, capable of assuming various reversible and interchangeable forms: motion, heat, magnetism, and electricity (Mayer 1984, pp. 85–95).

The mechanistic view of matter – with its predictability and rigid determinism – gradually evolved into one emphasizing the dynamic interaction of energy and fields. The study of light's dual behavior as both wave and particle revealed new insights into material phenomena. The discovery of electromagnetism introduced the abstract concept of the field, paving the way for unprecedented technological advances, such as the transmission of energy and information through radio waves across unimaginable distances.

Finally, the discoveries of Marie Curie (1867–1934) and Pierre Curie (1859–1906) in the 19th century demonstrated the "transmutation" of matter through radiation – alpha, beta, and gamma particles – revealing the instability of even the most solid elements of the material world.

From the 20th century onward, humanity has witnessed the emergence of increasingly powerful instruments that have expanded the range and precision of our senses – both for observing the micro and macro cosmos – enhancing our journey toward the vast and ever more "immaterial" universe.

The absolutism, certainties, and determinism of past centuries have faded away. Time, space, and matter are no longer what they once seemed. We now recognize how little we truly know of our greater dwelling – the Universe.

Foreseeing the growing advancements of science and its insatiable drive to explore the unknown, Allan Kardec declared:

> "Spiritism and Science complement each other reciprocally; Science, without Spiritism, finds itself unable to explain certain phenomena solely through the laws of matter; while Spiritism, without Science, would lack support and control. The study of the laws of matter had to precede that of spirituality, for matter is what first strikes the senses. If Spiritism had appeared before the scientific discoveries, it would have failed, like all things that come before their time." (*Kardec, 2013, p. 23*)

Let us consider, through a few examples, how our friends from the spiritual realm anticipated by more than a century some of today's scientific discoveries.

Concerning matter, Kardec asked in *The Spirits' Book*:

> "Is ponderability an essential attribute of matter?"
>
> "Of matter as you understand it, yes; but not of matter considered as universal fluid. The ethereal and subtle matter that constitutes this fluid is imponderable to you. Nevertheless, it is the principle of your dense, ponderable matter." (Kardec 2013, p. 64)

Today, we know that each of us is constantly traversed by about one trillion neutrinos per second – particles originating in the heart of the Sun and traveling at nearly the speed of light. These particles are practically imponderable and pass through almost everything; they could traverse a solid column of concrete stretching from our galaxy to the nearest one, Andromeda, without being detected – hence the name "ghost particles."

Furthermore, Einstein's theory of relativity revealed that time passes differently depending on the observer's state of motion. Time flows more slowly for an observer in motion than for one at rest, relative to a shared event – demonstrating that time is not absolute but relative, capable of being "stretched" depending on relative velocity.

This intrinsic property of nature has been repeatedly confirmed in experiments – for example, by comparing ultra-precise atomic clocks placed on airplanes with identical ones kept on the ground. For those in flight, time passes more slowly. *(*Júnior 2012*)*

Let us observe the fascinating dialogue recorded by Allan Kardec with the spirit of a pharmacist's father, named Georges, from a town in southern France – an exchange that beautifully illustrates the relativity of time (Kardec 2004, p. 46*):*

> Kardec: "What sensation did you experience when you left your corporeal envelope?"
>
> Spirit: "Disturbance."
>
> Kardec: "How long did this disturbance last?"
>
> Spirit: "Brief for me; long for you."
>
> Kardec: "Can you estimate the duration of this disturbance in our way of counting time?"
>
> Spirit: "Ten years for you; ten minutes for me."

This concise but profound communication hints at temporal relativity – a concept that science would only formalize decades later.

The final example concerns recent scientific advances – particularly in the last two decades – regarding the origin of the material (baryonic) universe. These discoveries belong to a specific field of quantum physics known as Quantum Chromodynamics (QCD).

Modern particle physics reveals that more than 99% of the visible universe's mass is composed of protons and neutrons. Each of these is, in turn, formed by three sub-particles called quarks, bound together by gluons – subatomic particles that act as a kind of "glue," responsible for the strong nuclear force that holds atomic nuclei together.

However, these three quarks and their gluons account for only about 1% of the mass of a proton or neutron. So, where does the remaining mass come from?

Scientists have discovered that the vast "emptiness" within atomic structures – the nucleus and its surrounding electron cloud – is not empty at all. Instead, it is filled with immaterial energy, formed by pairs of matter and antimatter particles that constantly fluctuate. According to Einstein's mass–energy equivalence equation ($E = mc^2$), during these fluctuations, fleeting particles arise with an incredibly short lifespan – on the order of one second divided by 10^{43}, an unimaginably brief duration that renders these particles practically unobservable, except through their indirect effects.

This energetic and immaterial "void," in fact, composed of these virtual particles, is known as the quantum vacuum. With its incessant energy fluctuations, it accounts for 99% of the remaining mass of matter. Thus, what we call vacuum – the notion of complete emptiness – does not exist in nature.

> Interestingly, the existence (or nonexistence) of the vacuum was a topic of heated debate in the 19th century. Let us recall *The Spirits' Book*, where Kardec asked this very question during that same era of scientific speculation:
>
> "Does absolute vacuum exist anywhere in universal space?"
>
> "No, there is no vacuum. What seems empty to you is occupied by matter that escapes your senses and instruments." *(*Kardec 2013, p. 66*)*

It is also interesting to note the characteristics of the quantum vacuum described above, which is present throughout the entire universe, permeating and filling everything that exists – from subatomic structures to intergalactic spaces. Let us observe the similarity between this and what the spiritual friends described as the Universal Cosmic Fluid:

> "There is an ethereal fluid that fills space and penetrates bodies. This fluid is the ether, or primitive cosmic matter, the generator of the world and of beings. Inherent to it are the forces that preside over the metamorphoses of matter – the immutable and necessary laws that govern the world." *(*Kardec 2013, p. 97*)*

Kardec placed great confidence in the principles presented by the enlightened spirits, knowing they were in better conditions to see the whole and to understand the broader framework of the universe:

> "Only stationary religions can fear the discoveries of Science, which are harmful only to those that allow themselves to be distanced by progressive ideas, immobilizing themselves in the absolutism of their beliefs. They generally form such a petty idea of Di-

> vinity that they cannot understand that assimilating the laws of nature, which Science reveals, is to glorify God through His works. In their blindness, however, such religions prefer to pay homage to the spirit of evil, attributing to it those very laws. A religion that, at no point, contradicts the laws of nature would have nothing to fear from progress and would be invulnerable." (Kardec 2013, p. 79)

All this knowledge about our home — Earth — and the vast journey through which we travel — the Universe — as well as that which will come in future centuries and millennia; the understanding of the unknowns that we still ignore, venturing into seas never before navigated, will surely allow science to arrive, perhaps unexpectedly, at the shores of the unimaginable spiritual world — radiant, magnificent, and indescribably beautiful.

When that moment comes, science and its researchers will defend these discoveries with such vigor and devotion that they may surpass the zeal shown by all religions and faith traditions throughout history.

Yet we must ask: is this our ultimate goal? Is our mission merely to marvel at the ever more indescribable beauty of creation and to delight in the experiences of our journey? Does it all have a purpose? And what of the traveler — do *we* not matter?

Could we, by doing so, reach the secrets of the First Cause — the Creator, the Divinity, God — and, welcomed into His intimacy, truly comprehend Him?

Imagine a book in your hands — beautiful, enchanting, and, one might say, magical. Now imagine yourself, like a fascinated child, studying it intently: its height, its width, the material of its pages, the trees from which the paper came, the number of pages. You go further, discovering in minute detail the characteristics of the pigment that forms the symbols you have named letters. You advance again, learning through intricate and almost secret formulas how these symbols are organized – the distances and angles that separate them, forming words, lines, and pages.

Would all this be enough to truly understand the book? And beyond that – would such knowledge allow you to know that the book had an author, and to comprehend that author?

As we have already been told, there is still a *sense* we lack.

And what sense is this?

We must learn to read.

In the Egyptian city of Luxor, within its namesake temple, one of the columns of the outer courtyard bears an inscription later adopted by the Greek sages:

"The body is the house of God."

> That is why it is said: "Human being, know yourself." (De Lubicz, Lamy & Har-Bak 1954)

Would this not be the very sense we lack—the knowledge of ourselves? And is it not within us that we would find the Author of this wondrous book of life? As the Master of Galilee affirmed:

"The Father is in me, and I am in the Father." (Dias 2013, p. 431)

And perhaps, knowing the disbelief of His beloved siblings and loving them so deeply, He repeated it so there would remain no doubt:

> "Do you not believe that I am in the Father and the Father is in me? The words I speak to you I do not speak on my own authority; rather, it is the Father, living in me, who does His work." (Dias 2013, p. 446)

It is in our relationship with the world—people, things, and ideas—that we come to know ourselves. In the active, nonjudgmental perception of these relationships, without demands or explanations, we learn to think and feel rightly. Thus, we come to know ourselves and move toward meeting the Creator, who awaits us with infinite patience and benevolence, within our very essence.

And when we are advanced in reading the open book of life, we will discover, in fascination, that it has no end. We are writing, and continue to write, many of its chapters; and without them, the book would remain incomplete.

Good reading, and good writing, dear friend.

Bibliography

DE LUBICZ, Isha S., Lucie Lamy, and Her-Bak. *The Living Face of Ancient Egypt.* London: Hodder and Stoughton, 1954.

JÚNIOR, Osvaldo P. "Experimentos relativísticos 2: paradoxo dos gêmeos em aviões." *Filosofia da Ciência.* Source:

http://opessoa.fflch.usp.br/sites/opessoa.fflch.usp.br/files/TR-Exp-2-Avioes.pdf. [Accessed January 1, 2021].

KARDEC, Allan. *Genesis.* USSF.

KARDEC, Allan. "A Conversion." *The Spiritist Review.* Brasília: USSF. (Year II, No. 13, January 1858).

MAYER, Julius R. "Observations on the Forces of Inanimate Nature." *Notebooks on the History and Philosophy of Science,* 6 (1984): 85–95.

SAINT-EXUPÉRY, Antoine de. *The Little Prince.* Rio de Janeiro: Agir, 2016.

André Luiz Peixinho Current President of the Spiritist Federation of the State of Bahia (FEEB), Brazil. (Deceased in 2024)

FROM KARDEC TO DENIS - A PHILOSOPHICAL APPROACH TO GOD

ANDRÉ LUIZ PEIXINHO

1. The nature of Spiritist knowledge and its production methodology in Kardec's work

Since the beginning of Spiritism, Allan Kardec proposed the alliance of science and religion when he published the seminal text of Spiritism – *The Spirits' Book* – presenting it as a spiritualist philosophy. He also made incursions into the interpretation of art, working with Spirits[31] who had dedicated themselves to it while incarnated. This method made him a pioneer in the reintegration of cultural spheres that had been separated in Modern times – spheres that had drifted so far apart as to become true antagonists – culminating in the hegemony of science in the nineteenth century.

Both the project of building Spiritist knowledge by interconnecting science, philosophy, religion, and art, and

31 Following what can be inferred from the special use that Allan Kardec makes of the spelling of the initial letter of the word *spirit* [compare, for example, question 23 and the note to question 76 of *The Spirits' Book* (Kardec 2020)], we will utilize lower case *s* for *spirit* when meaning the *universal intelligent element* - except in direct quotations, and capital *S* to designate individualized spiritual beings.

the constant presence of concepts opposing materialism and the dominant worldview of the nineteenth century, allow us to affirm, in contemporary terms, that Spiritism is, epistemologically, a paradigm or worldview that seeks to transcend the materialist doctrine, previously regarded as valid across almost all fields of knowledge.

This original approach to the creation of Spiritist knowledge becomes even more distinctive through its acceptance of revelation from the Spirits as a legitimate source of information, duly classified according to their level of evolution. This innovation inaugurated an era of collective knowledge production on an inter-existential basis.

These considerations lead us to understand that certain subjects can be thoroughly studied using methodologies from multiple cultural spheres. Reincarnation, for example, can be investigated scientifically, as Albert de Rochas did when he published *Successive Lives* (2002); philosophically, as presented in the chapter "Multiple Lives" in *The Spirits' Book*; through the palingenetic insights revealed and described by Léon Denis in *The Great Enigma: God and the Universe* (2019); through poetic narratives such as *Poetry from Beyond the Grave* (Xavier, 2013); and through numerous mediumistic novels, such as *Two Thousand Years Ago* (Xavier, 2011b), followed by *Fifty Years Later* (Xavier, 2011a), both dictated by the Spirit Emmanuel and psychographed by the medium Chico Xavier.

This multidimensional way of constructing knowledge is far more fruitful than any production derived from a single cultural sphere.

It is understandable, however, that each object of study may be better explored within one particular cultural domain, depending both on its inherent characteristics and on the analytical capacities of human beings at their current stage of progress – as is the case with the study of God. When it comes to God, the contributions of science remain indirect, focusing mainly on the analysis of the universe, and thus of limited relevance in a broader sense.

In our recent Western history, the subject has been treated primarily within philosophy, often absorbed by religion. Therefore, it is not surprising that Kardec and the Spirits emphasized this particular sphere of knowledge in order to make Spiritist understanding accessible through the means available in their time – especially in addressing one of philosophy's great problems: the concept of God.

An examination of philosophical trends reveals no consensus regarding their investigative method. Most employ the faculty of reason as a fundamental instrument for this endeavor. Yet reason itself has become an object of study, leading to diverse interpretations of its ability to generate valid knowledge. Kardec's predecessors – philosophers such as Descartes, Kant, and Leibniz – attributed varying degrees of importance and distinct functions to it. Pascal and the Romantic philosophers, on the other hand, favored the reasons of the heart – *l'esprit de finesse* – while later thinkers like Bergson elevated intuition as the preeminent faculty for philosophical inquiry.

A close study of the texts of the so-called Spiritist Codification, all edited by Allan Kardec, reveals several epistemological characteristics. For instance, in defining Spiritism, we can discern a deliberate preference for a positivist, empirical, and experimental – therefore scientific – approach. Nothing summarizes this choice better than the statement:

> "Spiritism is a science that deals with the nature, origin, and destiny of spirits, and their relation with the corporeal world." (Kardec 2011c, p. 48)

Yet, in making this choice, Kardec distinguishes between intelligent manifestations and their cultural content – the latter being consecrated as the philosophical part of Spiritism and of paramount importance in clarifying the destiny of humankind. Thus, *The Spirits' Book* begins with the designation *Spiritualist Philosophy.*

> We can see that this is a philosophy based in reason, similar to Occam's razor[32] regarding the experiences of faith, and which was marked by the aphorism: "unshakable faith is the kind that can stand face to face with reason in all human epochs" (Kardec 2011b, 315).

Since *reason* is a polysemic term, we may inquire as to which of its meanings Kardec is referring. According to Souza (2003, pp. 110-111), there are three basic meanings of the word:

a) it is the human faculty that differentiates humans from animals—the capacity for self-examination and reflection upon oneself;

b) it is equivalent to fundamentals, that is, the faculty to explain why something occurs in a certain way and not in another;

c) it corresponds to *logos*—reason as speech or discourse.

Souza adds:

> "From what we can infer from the passages indicated both in *The Gospel According to Spiritism* (Kardec 2011b) and in *Posthumous Works* (Kardec 1993), Kardec uses the word *reason* as a principle to explain realities—the logical way of thinking about facts, of

32 Economic principle of the scientific method used as a criterion to evaluate the quality of scientific theories, which consists in choosing the simplest explanation when deciding between two or more theoretical formulations.

discovering the connections between cause and effect."

This concept resembles the notion of *sufficient reason* defined by Leibniz, and it can be found in *The Spirits' Book*. Souza explains this use of reason as follows:

> "The three arguments that originate from sufficient reason were addressed in *The Spirits' Book*:
>
> a) the existence of something rather than nothing, because being is superior to non-being (comment on question 35);
>
> b) the inexistence of a vacuum in the universe, since it is impossible to explain why some parts would be occupied and others not (question 36);
>
> c) matter cannot be merely extension, for there would be no justification for it being more concentrated in one place than in another (question 22)." (Souza 2003, p. 211)

In conclusion, we understand that Kardec proposed a type of faith founded on facts (*empiricism*) and logic (*rationalism*), producing a faith whose results are verifiable—free from dogmas, religious absolutism, the hegemony of external rituals over genuine inner sentiment, and from doctrines that encourage blind acceptance or generate fanaticism. These were essential elements for restoring the role of religion in the cultural context of the time, when its reputation had been shaken by Enlightenment criticism, the rise of philosophical materialism, and emerging scientism.

From this introduction, we can infer that:

- Spiritism, as a body of knowledge, constitutes a cosmic vision, a universalist paradigm that includes and transcends materialism while reintegrating the cultural spheres;

- certain subjects of study are more closely associated with particular cultural spheres, such as God with Philosophy;
- Kardec employed reason—particularly *sufficient reason*—to validate Spiritist knowledge;
- Kardec also regarded divine revelation, accessed through faith, as a legitimate source of knowledge.

2. The Existence of God; God's Attributes; God's Relation with Creation According to the Spiritist Codification

2.1 Philosophical Evidences of the Existence of God

The very first question of *The Spirits' Book* asks: "What is God?" The way it is phrased already suggests the possibility of conceiving of God beyond the traditional anthropomorphic notion.

The answer provided is based on one of the fundamental assumptions of scientific inquiry: the principle of causality, a creation of reason. Every effect has a cause, and every intelligent effect must have an intelligent cause. Yet, to avoid an infinite regression in the search for the cause of the cause, it becomes necessary to admit the existence of an original Cause—a Cause that is self-existent and independent of anything else.

The answer given by the Spiritist Revelation is not new in philosophical terms. Since Aristotle, and later through Thomas Aquinas, philosophy has offered multiple arguments for the existence of God. In his Aristotelian-Thomistic synthesis, Thomas Aquinas formulated five logical expressions—known as the Five Ways—in favor of the existence of God: the Unmoved Mover, the First Cause, the Necessary Being, the Absolute Being, and the Grand

Designer (Sciacca 1967).

The Fifth Way, or *Grand Designer,* also appears among the proofs of God's existence in *The Spirits' Book,* as seen in the statement:

> "The harmony that regulates the universe can only result from predetermined combinations and ends, thereby revealing the existence of an intelligent power *[...]." (*Kardec 2020, p. 40*)*

> Another argument presented as evidence of God's existence is the recognition that belief in God is universal—present in all human faiths and *traditions (*Kardec 2020, pp. 39–40*)*.

When asked whether God is a distinct being or merely the sum of all the forces and intelligences of the universe, the Spirits clearly affirm that God has a distinct nature, thereby rejecting the pantheistic concept that equates God with Nature or with the Cosmos in its totality and infinity. Kardec reinforces this point:

> "God's intelligence is revealed in the work of creation, as an artist in his or her canvas. God's works are no more part of God than the canvas is the artist who painted it." *(*Kardec 2020, p. 43*)*

Even the Pure Spirits, who belong to the First Order of the Spiritist Hierarchy, are not to be confused with God:

> "They [Pure Spirits] are God's messengers and ministers, the executors of God's will in maintaining universal harmony." *(*Kardec 2020, p. 75*)*

2.2 Attributes of God

In the *Spiritist Codification,* the Spirits explain that we are not yet capable of understanding the essential nature of

God, since we have not yet developed the necessary senses or faculties to do so. This comprehension will only be possible when we reach complete purification. They emphasize that we should not waste our time on matters beyond our grasp, affirming that it would be far more useful to dedicate ourselves to self-improvement and to the wise use of the knowledge already available to us – knowledge that will place us in a better condition to understand God. By applying this knowledge in harmony with reason, we can deduce what God may be – and, more importantly, what the Divine Being absolutely cannot be.

Thus, in *The Spirits' Book* (Kardec 2020, p. 41) and *Genesis* (Kardec 2011a, pp. 63–65), Kardec identifies the following as attributes of God:

- God is the supreme and sovereign intelligence.
- God is eternal.
- God is immutable.
- God is immaterial.
- God is omnipotent.
- God is supremely just and good.
- God is infinitely perfect.
- God is unique.

To arrive at this list of attributes, Kardec employs the principle of negation – the impossibility of *non-being*. For example, God cannot be mutable, because if this were the case, the universal laws would lack consistency. Moreover, any change in God's nature – a transition from what God *is* to what God *is not yet* – would imply imperfection.

According to Kardec, these divine attributes serve as a secure standard for evaluating the truth of any theory, belief, or practice. Any claim that contradicts or diminishes even one of these essential attributes cannot be true:

> "In philosophy, psychology, ethics and religion there is nothing true except that which does not wander one iota from the essential qualities of the Divinity." (Kardec 2011a, p. 66)

2.3 God's Relationship with Creation

In a spiritual communication received from the Spirit Quinemant in 1867 and published in *Genesis* (Kardec, 2011a, pp. 69–70), Allan Kardec affirms that God is present everywhere – including in Nature. All the elements of Creation are in constant relationship with the Divine Being, as though the entirety of Creation were immersed in a divine fluid.

He explains:

> "Hence, we are constantly in the presence of the Divinity. There is not one of our actions that we may hide from its gaze. Our thought is in constant contact with its thought, and it is correct to say that God reads the deepest folds of our mind. We are in God just as God is in us, according to what Christ said." (Kardec 2011a, pp. 68–69)

2.4 The Human–God Relationship

It is through an innate sentiment that human beings recognize the existence of God. In perceiving the superiority of the Divine Being over all Creation, we are led to revere our Creator. Among all forms of worship, the most elevated is the one that originates in the heart.

Prayer is recognized as an act of worship through which we may praise, ask, and give thanks. Although prayer does not alter the laws of God – and although the Creator already knows what is best for each of us – it can influence those events that stem from free will (as opposed to those that are predetermined), and thus it operates without violating eternal law. Moreover, prayer transforms the mental and emotional state of those who pray, enabling them to attune with higher spiritual regions and entities that inspire and guide them in the decision-making processes of life.

***

From this set of reflections, we conclude that although Kardec employed the intellectual tools of his time – such as reason and empirical research – he did not confine himself to merely reproducing preexisting philosophical ideas. While he retrieved ancient hypotheses, he also validated them through *selective inter-existential information,* choosing spiritual sources that demonstrated wisdom and conveyed messages of convergent content.

Evidently, choosing reason as the supreme criterion for defining truth imposes certain boundaries that cannot be crossed. Therefore, in order to present the idea of God within a rational framework, Kardec adopted the concept of supreme intelligence, rather than that of ultimate sentiment or infinite beauty.

3. Denis: The Reconnection of Knowledge Fields and the Expansion of the Methodology of Knowledge About God

Considered by many Spiritists of his time and ours to be Allan Kardec's successor, Léon Denis—who met the Master of Lyon in his youth—declared himself to be his follower, as he affirmed in his own words:

> "That is why we proposed to adopt herein the terms, the views, the methods used by Allan Kardec as being the safest, while reserving the right to add to my

> work all the developments resulting from fifty years of research and experimentation that have passed since the release of his books." (Denis 2018, p. 40)

It is noteworthy that Denis emphasizes the possibility of progress within Spiritist ideas—an evolution already foreseen by Kardec—without, however, altering the foundational principles or structural framework of Spiritism. He also articulates what appears to be his vision for the future:

> "A day will come when all the small, narrow and old systems will merge into a vast synthesis embracing all the realms of the idea. Sciences, philosophies, religions which are today divided, will join in the light, and will become life, the splendor of the spirit, the reign of Knowledge. In this magnificent agreement, the sciences will provide precision and method in the order of facts; the philosophies, rigor in their logical deductions; poetry, the irradiation of its lights and the magic of its colors. Religion will add the qualities of feeling and the notion of high aesthetics." (Denis 2018, p. 33)

This vision reveals Denis' desire to continue the work of reconnecting the fields of knowledge, a project that, interestingly, is also pursued today within certain materialistic paradigms. He thus conceives of an integrative epistemology—an organic structure that rejects the hegemony of any single discipline, instead integrating diverse methods, sources, and cultural spheres into a holistic pursuit of truth.

Because Denis lived in a different era, was shaped by distinct cultural influences, and was guided by superior Spirits who had undergone their own unique experiences, he fulfilled his promise by identifying new means of acquiring knowledge: intuition, inner sense, and contemplation. While he engaged in rational analyses of Spiritist thought and explored inter-existential intellectual concepts, he simultaneously broadened the possibilities of Spiritist gnosis.

In the realm of philosophical studies, Denis shared with his contemporary Henri Bergson the conviction that intelligence alone cannot fully grasp life and evolution. Referring to Bergson's approach, Denis observed:

> "What did he [Bergson] do? He replaced intelligence with intuition, and this is an event of the highest importance in Psychology." (Denis 2011, p. 138)

Regarding the inner senses, Denis identified **introspection** as the best method for reaching transcendental truths:

> "It is through their inner senses that human beings perceive transcendental facts and truths. (...) It is this deep, unknown sense, unused by most humans, that some experimenters have referred to as the subliminal consciousness." (Denis 2018, p. 381)

Here, Denis expands the French philosophical tradition, which favors inner observation, in contrast to English empiricism. In the 19th century, before Bergson, this intellectual lineage had already been influenced by the writings of Maine de Biran, later popularized through the eclecticism of Victor Cousin (Sciacca 1967, p. 97).

As for contemplation, Denis became a true master of this Gnostic discipline, producing exquisite reflections on Nature, especially in his attempts to "study" God. These meditative lessons are found throughout *The Big Enigma.*

During his lifetime, evolutionism, in its various forms, had become deeply rooted in culture. Denis adopted this structuring principle—already present in *The Spirits' Book*—to demonstrate that our modes of perception, and therefore our conceptions of God, also evolve. In a masterful synthesis of this evolution, he wrote:

> "Viewed through the prism of his senses, God is multiple: all of nature's forces are gods, thus poly-

theism was born. Considered by the intellect, God is manifold, spirit and matter: hence arises duality. To pure reason He appears triple: soul, mind and body. This conception has given birth to the Trinitarian religions of India and to Christianity. Perceived by the will... God is Unique and Absolute. In God the three fundamental principles of the universe combine to compose one living unity." *(*Denis 2017, p. 116*)*

In summary, perception depends on the evolutionary level of the perceiving being; the faculties of knowledge evolve alongside the spirit itself.

The proofs of God's existence, as a result of this expansion of Gnostic possibilities, have multiple origins. In Denis' writings, we find acceptance of the principle of causality and of the ordering intelligence revealed to Kardec by the Spirits. Denis also revives Aristotle's notion of the Unmoved Mover, while adding evidence derived from:

- the study of the laws of Nature,
- the moral truths revealed by conscience, and
- the ideal beauty that inspires all art.

He recognizes that at the heart of all these inquiries lies the conception of a necessary and perfect Being, the supreme source of Goodness, Beauty, Truth, and Justice.

Thus, Denis promotes a methodological expansion in the search for philosophical evidence of God's existence. His inclusion of Beauty as a path toward the Divine Presence is particularly striking. In this sense, his work renews the great Platonic tradition and reflects a Kantian influence in his treatment of moral conscience, integrating these philosophical legacies within a broader Spiritist framework.

3.1 The Attributes of God

In Denis's work, we perceive the affirmation of God's attributes as taught in the Spiritist Codification, expressed in a more poetic and literary language, and complemented by new nuances—such as the inclusion of love as a divine attribute. The following excerpts from *The Big Enigma* (Denis 2019) illustrate this expanded vision:

> "Creator! Source of all wisdom and love..." (Denis 2019, p. 36)
>
> "To pray is to turn ourselves toward the eternal Being..." (Denis, 2019, pp. 75–76)
>
> "...source of eternal justice..." (Denis 2019, p. 60)
>
> "...the supreme Cause brings everything back to order and harmony." (Denis 2019, p. 60)
>
> "God hovers above everything." (Denis 2019, p. 51)
>
> "God is the spirit of wisdom, love and life, the infinite power that governs the world." (Denis 2019, p. 27)
>
> "God, being perfection itself, cannot be limited." (Denis 2019, p. 88)

3.2 God and Creation

In a distinct literary style, Denis (*2017*) reaffirms God's presence in the world as its creator and sustaining essence, declaring:

> "The self of the universe is God: the Supreme Unity..." (Denis 2017, p. 353)
>
> "God is infinite and cannot be individualized—that is to say, separated from the world." (Denis 2017, p. 104)
>
> "The Supreme Being does not exist outside of the

> world, of which God is the essential and integral part." (Denis 2017, p. 112)
>
> "God is in us, or at least there is a reflection of God in us." (Denis 2017, p. 115)
>
> "...the infinite and absolute being by itself becomes relative and finite with its creatures..." (Denis 2017, pp. 117–118)

In *The Big Enigma* (2019, p. 34), Denis adds:

> "This universe, which God has peopled with intelligences, so that they may know It, love It and fulfill Its law, while filling themselves with Its presence, and suffusing themselves with Its light warmed by Its endless love."

Initially, Denis approaches the relationship between God and Creation somewhat differently from Kardec. In his commentary on Question 16 of *The Spirits' Book* (*Kardec, 2020, p. 43*), Kardec uses the analogy of a painter and their painting, stressing the distinction between the two. Later, he considers that God is present in all Nature, and that all Nature is immersed in the divine fluid (Kardec 2011a, p. 68). Denis's conception—God as the soul or self of the universe—is therefore closer to this latter view, while also rejecting pantheism, as Kardec did.

For both authors, prayer is presented as the primary means of connection with the Divine, described in nearly identical terms regarding its purposes of praise and supplication. Extending this notion to the creative act, Denis writes:

> "The life of a good individual is a continual prayer, a perpetual communion with fellow beings and with God." (Denis 2019, p. 35)
>
> "To work with a lofty feeling, by pursuing a useful and generous goal, is still to pray." (Denis 2019, p. 35)

4. Conclusion

As final reflections, certain guiding questions must be posed. As Kardec foresaw, Spiritist knowledge has progressed—yet problems and their solutions are always framed by the times and the maturity of those who address them. More than 150 years after Kardec's writings and a century after Denis's publications, it is worth asking: How are we advancing in the methodology of knowledge production? To what extent are we continuing the ambitious project of reintegrating the cultural spheres that Kardec initiated and Denis expanded?

The importance we place on God also warrants renewed reflection. The authors we have examined—both inspired by enlightened Spirits and writing in distinct idioms—converge on the same summit of human evolution: the full communion of the soul with God. We may, therefore, undertake a valuable exercise of self-examination by observing our personal awareness of the Supreme Being and its resonance in our daily lives.

Finally, as Spiritists who strive to revive the teachings of the Gospel as an integral part of Spiritism's mission, in harmony with Kardec and the Spirits of the Codification, we may find inspiration in the prayer of Jesus, offered for those who would believe in Him through His message:

> "My prayer is not for them alone. I pray also for those who will believe in me through their message, that all of them may be one, Father, just as you are in me and I am in you. May they also be in us so that the world may believe that you have sent me.
>
> I have given them the glory that you gave me, that they may be one as we are one — I in them and you in me — so that they may be brought to complete unity. Then the world will know that you sent me and have loved them even as you have loved me."*(John 17:20 23, NIV)*

Bibliography

DENIS, Léon. *After Death.* Translated by George G. Fleurot (1909) and Jussara Korngold (2017). New York: United States Spiritist Council, 2017. Kindle edition.

———. *The Big Enigma: God and the Universe.* Translated by Helton Mattar Monteiro. New York: United States Spiritist Council, 2019.

———. *O Mundo Invisível e a Guerra* [*The Invisible World and the War*]. Rio de Janeiro: CELD, 2001.

———. *The Problems of Life and Destiny: Experimental Studies.* Translated by Helton Mattar Monteiro. New York: United States Spiritist Council, 2018. Kindle edition.

KARDEC, Allan. *Genesis – Miracles and Predictions According to Spiritism.* Translated by Darrel W. Kimble and Ily Reis. Brasília: International Spiritist Council, 2011a.

———. *The Gospel According to Spiritism.* Translated by Darrel W. Kimble and Ily Reis. 2nd ed. Brasília: International Spiritist Council, 2011b.

———. *Obras Póstumas* [*Posthumous Works*]. Translated to Portuguese by Elias Barbosa. 1st ed. Araras: IDE, 1993.

———. *The Spirits' Book: The Principles of Spiritism.* Translated by the USSF [Nicole Alves]. 3rd rev. ed. New York: United States Spiritist Council / United States Spiritist Federation, 2020. Kindle edition.

———. *What Is Spiritism?* Translated by Darrel Kimble, Marcia Saiz, and Ily Reis. 2nd ed. Brasília: International Spiritist Council, 2011c.

ROCHAS, Albert de. *As Vidas Sucessivas* [*Successive Lives*]. Bragança Paulista: Lachâtre, 2002.

SCIACCA, Michele F. *História da Filosofia, Vol. II* [*History of Philosophy, Vol. II*]. São Paulo: Mestre Jou, 1967.

SOUZA, Elzio F., from the Spirit Yogashririshnam. *Divina Presença* [*Divine Presence*]. Salvador: Circulus, 2003.

XAVIER, Francisco C., from Various Spirits. *Poetry from Beyond the Grave.* Translated by Vitor Pequeno and Jeremy Fernando. Tielt: Uitgeverij, 2013.

———, from the Spirit Emmanuel. *Fifty Years Later.* Translated by Amy Duncan, Darrel Kimble, and Ily Reis. Brasília: International Spiritist Council, 2011.

———, from the Spirit Emmanuel. *Two Thousand Years Ago.* Translated by Amy Duncan, Darrel Kimble, and Ily Reis. 2nd ed. Brasília: International Spiritist Council, 2011.

Laudelino Risso Physiotherapist, Osteopath, Trained in Mind and Body Medicine, Trained in Evaluation and treatment of pain: principles and practice of pain medicine. Specialist in manual therapy. Podoposturology Training.

GOD, PRINCIPLE OF ETERNITY

LAUDELINO RISSO

How can we define te indefinable? How can we limit the unlimited, find cause among primary causes, or seek origin in what is eternal?

The concepts of understanding God evolve with the advancement of humanity, yet this does not mean that God changes.

> "Human language is powerless to say it, because there is no point of comparison for us to give us an idea of such a thing. We are like the blind from birth to those who uselessly sought to make us understand the brightness of the Sun." (Kardec 2013, 61)

The intellectual, emotional, and spiritual maturation of the human being awakens the indelible conscience according to the achievements of self-individuality and self-effort. With each new stage of progress arises a new understanding of the same subject.

When we think about love and attempt to define it, we do so according to our own experiences, which occur at different levels of maturity—causing both the response and the understanding to change over time. The same applies to our comprehension of God.

> "Beloved, let us love one another, for love comes from God. Everyone who loves is born of God and knows God. Whoever does not love does not know God, because God is love." (1 John 4:7–8)
>
> "God is, in principle, elementary to those who think of a cause by its effects, even if the cause is unseen. Science goes further: it calculates the power of the cause by the power of the effect, and can even determine its nature."
>
> "So is the universal mechanism: God does not show Itself, but affirms Itself through Its works." (Kardec 2003, 51)

From a materialist point of view, the agglutination of the masses that generated the Big Bang occurred through gravitational, magnetic, and electrical forces inherent to the universe itself. As Stephen Hawking states:

> "Because there is a law such as gravity, the universe can and will create itself from nothing. Spontaneous creation is the reason there is something rather than nothing, why the universe exists, why we exist." (Hawking 2010, 97)

This view implies that it would not be necessary to postulate a God for such a phenomenon. However, we perceive the limitation of such a narrow analysis, which judges the effect without considering the true cause. If there are forces responsible for the motion of molecules, these forces must have a causal agent. Therefore, if motion is an intelligent effect, it must originate from an equally intelligent cause.

To establish solid foundations for reflection on the understanding of what God is, this article invites the reader to explore the secure grounds of religion, science, and philosophy.

> "In Nature, everything vibrates in harmonic chords, under conditions determined by an intelligence. However, the laws from which this harmony results are superior to it, for the cause is always greater than the effect.
>
> It is because of God that the universes are formed, that the celestial bodies display their dazzling splendors in the immensities of infinity. It is because of God that the planets gravitate in space around luminous foci, forming radiant halos of suns.
>
> God is the eternal, immense, indefinable life—the Beginning and the End, the Alpha and the Omega. It is God who, in the abyss of time, willed the universe to exist, and the cosmic dust began to move. By God's will, the admirable laws of matter unfold the infinite and wonderful combinations that produce all that exists." (Bodier & Regnauld 2001, 78)

It is not a matter of defining God—an impossible task, for one cannot confine the infinite—but rather of reflecting on facts and history in order to approach an ever-broadening comprehension of the Divine.

The Theory of Evolution presented by Charles Darwin (1859) challenged faith built upon fragile foundations, refuting the mythical explanations of a God who, according to ancient beliefs, had formed woman from a man's rib—an interpretation unable to withstand the scrutiny of reason. By presenting the natural evolution of species, Darwin was accused of causing the "death of God," as his theory demonstrated that the diversity of life followed natural laws.

At the same time, Alfred Russel Wallace—often cited by Darwin—developed his own evolutionary perspective. Through his research and writings on the spirit and its immortality, Wallace sought to illuminate minds still trapped in ignorance, presenting the spiritual principle as a real and essential component in the logical reasoning of evolution, and above all, in the conception of a just and loving God.

Later, in *Man and Evolution*, Wallace asserted:

> "Natural selection cannot justify mathematical, artistic, or musical genius, nor metaphysical contemplation, reason, or humor. Something in the invisible universe of Spirit must have intervened at least three times in history: (1) in the creation of life from inorganic matter;
>
> (2) in the emergence of consciousness in higher animals;
>
> (3) in the generation of the faculties of the human spirit." (Smith 1922, 159)

In 1865, Wallace investigated the phenomena of "turning tables" through the mediumship of Marshall, Cuppy, and others, later affirming that communications with spirits "are as fully proven as any facts accepted in other sciences." (Smith 1922, 131)

In 1857, when *The Spirits' Book* was published in France, its author—Professor Rivail, under the pseudonym Allan Kardec—reframed the traditional question about God. Rather than asking *"Who is God?"*, he asked *"What is God?"*—a formulation that demonstrates the depth of his reasoning and opened the way for a clearer understanding of the Divine:

> "What is God? God is the Supreme Intelligence, the Primary Cause of all things." (Kardec 2001, 51)

Although it is impossible to update Kardec's thought or the wisdom of the Superior Spirits who collaborated in this monumental work, we find in question 13 of *The Spirits' Book* a synthesis of the attributes of Divinity, allowing us to draw closer to the understanding of the Creator:

> "When we state that God is eternal, infinite, immutable, immaterial, one, all-powerful, and supremely just and good, do we not have a complete idea of God's attributes? From your own point of view, yes, because you believe that in so stating them you have named them all. Nevertheless, you should understand that there are things that transcend the intelligence of even the most enlightened minds—things your language cannot define, for it is limited by your ideas and sensations.
>
> Your reason tells you that God must be perfect in these attributes to the highest degree; for if God lacked any of them, or was not perfect in them, God would not be superior to all things and therefore would not be God. To be superior to all things, God must be unchangeable and perfect in every conceivable way."

God is eternal. If God had a beginning, then either God would have had to spring from nothing or would have had to be created by a being that existed previously. By reasoning in this way, we gradually arrive at the idea of eternity and infinity.

God is immutable. If God were subject to change, the laws governing the universe would have no stability.

God is immaterial. This means that God's nature differs from everything we call matter; otherwise, God would not be immutable but would be subject to the transformations of matter.

God is one. If there were several gods, there would be no unity of design or power in the organization of the universe.

God is all-powerful because God is one. If God were not more powerful than everything else, it would mean that there was something as powerful or even superior. It would also imply that God might not have created all things, and that those which God did not create would have had to be the work of another god.

God is supremely just and good. The providential wisdom in the divine laws is revealed in the smallest things as well as in the largest, and this wisdom makes it impossible for us to doubt either God's justice or God's goodness. (Kardec 2001, 54–55)

Despite recognizing all these attributes of the Godhead as realities, the human being still finds great difficulty in understanding the Eternal—an explanation found in *Genesis*, in which the Spirit Quinemant declares:

> "The human being is a tiny world, where the director is the Spirit and the directed principle is the body. In this world, the body represents a creation, of which the Spirit represents God (keep in mind that this refers only to a question of similarity, not identity). The parts of this body—the different organs that compose it, such as muscles, nerves, and joints—are other material individualities located at specific points of the body.
>
> Although the number of these constituent parts, so varied and different in nature, is considerable, no one questions the fact that no movement may occur or that any impression may be produced at any point without the Spirit being aware of it. Are there simultaneous sensations at many points?
>
> The Spirit senses, discerns, and analyzes all of them, assigning to each one its cause and location, through the intermediary of the perispiritual fluid.
>
> An analogous phenomenon occurs between God and Creation. God is everywhere in Nature, just as

> the spirit is everywhere in the body. All the elements of creation are in constant relation with God, in the same way that all the cells of the human body are in direct contact with the spiritual being.
>
> Thus, there is no reason why phenomena of the same order should not occur in an identical manner in both cases.
>
> A limb moves: the spirit senses it. A creature thinks: God knows about it. All limbs are in movement; the various organs are in motion; the spirit senses each manifestation, distinguishes it, and locates it. The different creations and creatures move, think, and act in diverse ways, and God knows everything that happens, assigning to each one what is particular to it.
>
> From this, one may also deduce the solidarity between matter and intelligence, the solidarity among all beings of a world and of all worlds, and, finally, the unity of all creation with the Creator." (Kardec 2013, 57–58)

Within the intimacy of every being lies the yearning to find, feel, and perceive God. This quest is beautifully symbolized in Michelangelo's masterpiece *The Creation of Adam,* painted on the ceiling of the Sistine Chapel. In this work of art—universally recognized as one of humanity's greatest achievements—we observe the hands of God and man approaching but not yet touching, inviting profound reflection. The image suggests that while the Creator extends Himself toward the creature, it is the human being who must make the final effort to bridge the remaining distance. A simple movement—a single gesture of the fingers—would be enough for contact to occur. Yet the initiative must come from the creature, not from the Creator.

In the 17th century, the emerging Enlightenment projected light into the dark abyss of ignorance, breaking the bonds imposed by the dominant Church, which maintained control over the State, science, and the conscience of those who placed their faith in God. Those who wished to have any connection with the Divine Entity were expected to strictly follow the rules—often misunderstood—that the Church imposed.

Voltaire tells us that:

> "God exists as the most credible thing that humans can conceive, and at the same time as one of the most absurd. I exist; therefore, something exists. If there is anything, it has existed from all eternity, because that which exists is either by itself or receives its being from another. If it is by itself, it necessarily has always existed, and it is God. I do not believe in the god that men created, but in the God that created men." (Voltaire 1978, 278)

From Copernicus to Galileo Galilei, the confrontation between scientists and the religious authorities intensified. This struggle gained new fuel with Friedrich Nietzsche's proclamation in *The Gay Science*:

> "God is dead! God remains dead! And we have killed him!" (Nietzsche 1882, 137)

The pessimistic philosopher expressed a rupture that great thinkers sought to address through deism, seeking to understand God through reason, freedom of thought, and science—rejecting the dogmatic structure of religion that ruled philosophy and the sciences through rituals and faith devoid of reason. This rupture freed knowledge from the control of religious institutions, enabling science to advance through multiple discoveries without the need for state or ecclesiastical approval.

Yet even today, in academic settings, we still perceive traces of this long history of oppression. Disciplines that study the soul—such as psychology, psychiatry, and other branches of the sciences—often hesitate to use the term *God* or *Divine psyche.* This hesitation stems from the fear of reviving the image of a punitive and authoritarian deity once imposed by religion. However, the concept defended by many philosophers and scientists remains: the recognition of a connection between the human being and the Divine, between the creature and the Creator.

Contemporary thought increasingly demonstrates that the universality of teachings now bridges the gaps left by centuries of misunderstanding. Terms such as *spirituality, religiosity, gratitude, compassion,* and *transcendence* have gained renewed relevance, not only in philosophical and ethical discussions but also in scientific research, where their therapeutic and psychological effectiveness has been empirically validated.

In *The God Gene,* Harvard geneticist Dr. Dean Hamer demonstrates that an individual's capacity for transcendence is linked to genetic inheritance, though it can also be developed through the process of self-discovery.

Hamer's research identified the VMAT2 gene (of numerical order 33050, located on chromosome 10), associated with moments when we transcend material reality and connect with the Divine through nature, acts of charity, or expressions of solidarity. In these moments, the brain produces up to four monoamines—instead of the normal two—including dopamine, serotonin, and oxytocin, hormones essential to emotional balance and well-being.

To disregard divine reality is to judge an effect without considering its cause. Both in academia and in life, the presence of God is a fact. Spiritist science offers tools to build a rational and experiential understanding of this reality, reconnecting the individual with the Creator—through the lenses of science and philosophy, but above all through love. For this is true religion: the living experience of God.

Bibliography

BODIER, Paul e Henri Regnauld. 2001. *Gabriel Delanne, Sua Vida, seu apostolado e sua obra.* Rio de Janeiro: Editora CELD.

HAMMER, Dean. 2005. *The God Gene.*

HAWKING, Stephen e Leonard Mlodinov. 2011. *The Grand Design: New answers to the ultimate questions of life.*

KARDEC, Allan. 2013. *Genesis.*: USSF/ISC.

KARDEC, Allan. 1999. *Instruções Práticas sobre as manifestações espíritas.* [Tradução Júlio Abreu Filho]. São Paulo: Editora Pensamento. Disponível em

http://www.autoresespiritasclassicos.com/Allan%20Kardec/Allan%20kardec%20Instrucoes%20Praticas/Allan%20Kardec%20-%20Instru%C3%A7%C3%B5es%20Pr%C3%A1ticas%20Sobre%20as%20Manifesta%C3%A7%C3%B5es%20Esp%C3%ADritas%20-%20Ano%201858.pdf

[consulted on 07/16/2020].

KARDEC, Allan, 2001. *The Spirits' Book.*: USSF/ISC.

KARDEC, Allan. 2004. *The Spiritist Review*: 1866 USSF.

NIETSCHE, Fiedrich. 1882. *A Gaia e a Ciência.* [Tradução Antonio Carlos Braga]. Disponível em

https://www.netmundi.org/home/wp-content/uploads/2017/05/Nietzsche-Friedrich-A-gaia-ciencia.pdf. [consultado em 12/05/2020].

SMITH, Charles H. 1992. *Alfred Russel Wallace on Spiritualism, Man & Evolution: Analytical Essay.* Torrington.

Disponível em https://people.wku.edu/charles.smith/essays/ARWPAMPH.htm [consulted on 04/25/2020].

VOLTAIRE. 1978. *Tratado de Metafísica 2.* São Paulo: Editora São Paulo.

Sílvia Almeida member of the association *No Invisível – Estudos e Divulgação Espírita*, Lisbon, Portugal. Collaborator with the Portuguese Spiritist Federation and with the Spiritist Social Communication Department of the CEI.

UNIVERSAL SOLIDARITY AND THE ETERNAL SPLENDOR OF CREATION

Or Humboldt and the researchers' vertigo.

SÍLVIA ALMEIDA

> "[...] The great forces that animate the universe proclaim the reality of divine intelligence; beside them, the majesty of God has been manifested in history by the action of great souls who, like huge tidal waves, bring to earthly shores all the powers generated by deeds of wisdom and love." *(Denis 2019, 17)*

Six years after declaring his intention to publish his life's work for the first time, Alexander von Humboldt (1769–1859) had still not sent the manuscript of the first volume to his publisher. Whenever frustration overtook him, he would leave his books and papers untouched on his desk and walk to the observatory, located about two miles from his home in Berlin, to gaze through the large telescope—where the universe revealed itself in all its splendor.

There, before the outpouring of twinkling stars, distant nebulae, and artfully painted planets—moments of profound beauty—he would find the inspiration he needed to continue.[33] (Wulf 2015, 550–51)

About four decades earlier, in 1804—the year Hippolyte Léon Denizard Rivail was born and Napoleon Bonaparte was crowned at Notre-Dame de Paris—Humboldt had returned from one of the most extraordinary scientific expeditions of all time: a five-year journey across the American continent.[34] He returned to Europe carrying dozens of notebooks, hundreds of drawings, thousands of astronomical, geological, and meteorological observations, and thousands of plant specimens—some of which were still unknown to European botanists (Wulf 2015, 256). This exuberant legacy would occupy the researcher for the next three decades, as he devoted himself to writing thirty volumes of scientific work.[35]

After that, Humboldt declared: "The mad frenzy has seized me of representing in a single work the whole material world."

33 See Wulf, "The Invention of Nature", 550-51.

34 Between 1799 and 1804, Humboldt crossed present-day Venezuela, Colombia, Ecuador, Peru, Cuba and Mexico, with the authorization of King Carlos IV of Spain, having covered a total of 5,996 miles on foot, on horseback or in canoes. During his navigation, he made observations in the areas of astronomy, meteorology and magnetism, as well as measured the temperature and chemical composition of the sea. He collected several specimens of unknown animals and plants, improved maps, took meticulous notes of the temperatures of rivers, soil and air, as well as atmospheric pressure, magnetic inclination, longitude and latitude. For the first time, nature was presented as a global force with the corresponding climatic zones throughout continents. An integrated world, where everything interacts.

35 Humbolt's book *Views of Nature,* one of the works resulting from the expedition to the Americas, would inspire several generations of scientists and poets. Charles Darwin read and reread it several times throughout his life, highlighting and taking notes in each of his copies, at each new reading, as if it were his first time. Darwin's expedition aboard the Beagle happened on account of Humboldt. Jules Verne, who had read all of Humboldt's books, was inspired by his adventures and quoted him in his works. Captain Nemo, from the *Twenty Thousand Leagues Under the Sea,* had Humboldt's complete work. Wulf, *The Invention of Nature,* 307-8.

At the age of sixty-five, he began what he considered to be his most influential book: *Cosmos: A Sketch of the Physical Description of the Universe*, which he described as "a sword in the breast that now has to be drawn" (Wulf 2015, 536–37).

To carry out this monumental task, Humboldt assembled an army of collaborators, all experts in their respective fields, which created a continuous influx of knowledge reaching Berlin over many months. These materials had to be analyzed, understood, and incorporated, causing the total body of data to grow and multiply endlessly—giving the impression of a task almost impossible to complete.

In addition to the materials he received, he relied on his own observations, many drawn from his numerous expeditions—from Chimborazo (in the equatorial Andes, then thought to be the highest mountain in the world, explored during his travels in the Americas) to the Caspian Sea (in Asia, investigated during his Central Asian expedition).

The writing of *Cosmos*'s five volumes occupied the last twenty-five years of his life. They were intended to unite everything in the heavens and on Earth, "ranging from distant nebulae to the geography of mosses, and from landscape painting to the migration of human races and poetry" (Wulf 2015, 536). It was a book about Nature, and as such, it aimed to evoke an impression as powerful and overwhelming as Nature itself, which he loved unconditionally.

Cosmos explored the "wide range of creation" (Wulf 2015, 537), addressing an extraordinary variety of subjects. It was not, however, an encyclopedic compilation like Diderot's *Encyclopédie*, for Humboldt sought instead to reveal the connections found in the "never-ending activity of the animated forces," linked through a "wonderful web of organic life" (Wulf 2015, 560–62).

At a time when science often stripped Nature of its enchantment by methodically uncovering its secrets, Humboldt remained convinced that Nature's splendor would forever inspire "excitement, astonishment, and wonder" (Wulf 2015, 560) – no matter how thoroughly it was described or explained.

In 1911, Léon Denis wrote about the universe:

> "It is the majesty of a mysterious power, of an intelligence that does not impose itself, but rather hides itself in the midst of things, revealing its presence to thought and to our hearts, and attracting the seeker like an infinite abyss." (Denis 2019, 15)

This description fits Humboldt perfectly. A scientist before the term even existed, he embodies the researcher's vertigo before the majesty of an intelligence that strikes both mind and heart. Yet, rather than "thought and heart," Humboldt preferred the terms intelligence and imagination – the latter evoking not irrational fancy, but the realm of feeling and intuition[36], bringing his perspective remarkably close to that of Denis.'

Humboldt's attraction to the wonders of the universe, encompassing both the macrocosm and the microcosm, is undeniable. From a very early age, he felt a kind of feverish restlessness – an irrepressible urge to explore the world. His insatiable thirst for knowledge led him to devote a significant portion of his inheritance to the American expedition, undertaken as soon as he was freed from the obligation of following his mother's wishes.

36 Following the flow of the Kantian ideas that reached him, in part, via Goethe. It was the emphasis on individual perception and subjectivity that allowed Humboldt to link the mechanistic view of nature to the poetry of the Romantics, which equipped him with 'new organs' with which to approach the natural world. See Wulf, *The invention of Nature,* 96-7.

We can better understand this exuberant drive when we learn, through Allan Kardec's research, about the origin of Humboldt's spirit, the mission he had embraced, and the connection he maintained with Earth.

Having decided to evoke Humboldt only a few days after his death[37], Kardec communicated with his spirit during the sessions of the Parisian Society for Spiritist Studies on May 13 and 20, 1859.

Their exchange was published in the Spiritist Review of June of the same year, under the heading: *Family Conversations from Beyond the Grave: Mr. Humboldt.*[38] Completely free from any material influence, Humboldt stated that his previous incarnation had taken place in a very distant world, unknown to terrestrial astronomers and superior to Earth:

> "It is far from you if you take into account your distances, the worldly measures. However, it is close if you use God's ruler and if, with a single gaze, you try to embrace the whole Creation." (Kardec 2016, 278)

He described it as a happy world, inhabited by benevolent spirits:

> "Nothing hinders the development of good thoughts there; nothing stimulates the recollection of bad ones. It is complete happiness, for everyone is con-

37 Humboldt passed away on May 6, 1859. His funeral ceremony in Berlin comprised a procession of mourners that was about a mile long.

38 As an addendum to the main subject of this article, it's interesting to note that one of the most used article titles in the *Spiritist Review* was "Family Conversations from Beyond the Grave", sometimes also named "Conversations from Beyond the Grave". Being practically a monthly item in the first years, it appears less and less often throughout the history of the *Review,* until disappearing completely from its table of contents in 1867. It is likely that, after the first few years of the *Review,* Allan Kardec considered that the study of the subject was complete, or perhaps that the evocations made afterwards did not add new information to the data they had obtained and published until that point.

> tent with themselves and with those who surround them. With regard to matter and the senses, any description would be useless. How simplified are the mechanisms of society there! Now that I am capable of comparing the two, I am astonished by the distance. Do not think that I say this to discourage you—quite the contrary. Your spirit must be deeply convinced of the existence of such worlds; then you will feel an ardent desire to reach them, and your work will pave the way." (Kardec 2016, 277)

Humboldt revealed that he was happy to have conscientiously fulfilled his mission, one of service to humankind. Several spirits, he said, had volunteered for this task—to share a portion of their abundance with those in need:

> "One does not give to the rich. I wanted to give; therefore, I came to the poor's dwelling." (Kardec 2016, 277)

He also expressed immense joy in his present condition and reverence for God. By the way he expressed himself, one recognizes a superior spirit, surrendered to the magnificence of the Creator and endowed with a comprehensive vision of Creation. His knowledge transcended all human reference, which explains why his way of perceiving and thinking about the world during his earthly life was so exceptionally unique.

Johann Wolfgang von Goethe (1749-1832) who, evoked by Allan Kardec, reported that he had also came to Earth from another sphere on a mission[39], felt amazed by the intellectual brilliance of Humboldt, of whom he was

39 Goethe was evoked at the *Parisian Society for Spiritist Studies* on March 25, 1856. His interview was published in the *Spiritist Review* of June 1859. The planet from which Goethe came was probably less evolved than Humboldt's. See: Kardec, *The Spiritist Review - 1859,* 284.

a very close friend.[40] Goethe always emerged invigorated after each visit Humboldt paid him, and said that his friend would make him dizzy with ideas; that "he had never met anyone so versatile", whose drive "whipped the scientific things with such speed that it was sometimes hard to follow." (Wulf 2015, 79-80)

Albert Gallatin (1761–1849), Thomas Jefferson's Secretary of the Treasury[41], recounted that Humboldt spoke incessantly, at twice the speed of anyone he knew. One could learn more from two hours of conversation with him than from two years of reading, Gallatin said, describing him as "a fountain of knowledge which flows in copious streams" (Wulf 2015, 238).

Humboldt spoke in German, English, French, and Spanish, often mixing them within the same speech, yet somehow making perfect sense—as though words themselves struggled to keep pace with the processing speed of his extraordinary intellect (Wulf 2015, 238).

Some of his ideas were so unconventional that even his translator felt compelled to add notes questioning their validity. In fact, several of those concepts have only recently been scientifically confirmed, such as the problem of deforestation and other environmental concerns (Wulf 2015, 492–93).

For a while, Humboldt was forced to stay in Berlin to entertain the intellect of the king, because he had spent

40 Humboldt had a kind of magnetizing, contagious personality. The period in which he and Goethe kept in touch was one of the most productive in the life of the German poet. When he was with Humboldt, "his mind worked in all directions." It was Humboldt who advised him to publish his research on comparative anatomy, and *Faust* was partly written during periods of bursts of activity, coinciding with his friend's visits. There are even those who find similarities between Faust and Humboldt, in their unstoppable and frantic search for knowledge. Wulf, *The Invention of Nature,* 76-7 and 94.

41 As with Goethe, who had found in Humboldt a partner to match his reflections, Jefferson immediately related with Humboldt. He, too, moved comfortably around science, being obsessed with measurements, records and data collection.

all of his inheritance money on his scientific studies, and his patron (Friedrich Wilhelm III, king of Prussia, who had financed Humboldt's time in Paris for years, while he was finishing the volumes related to his American expedition) had run out of patience[42]. Less than six months after arriving in that profoundly boring and not at all stimulating (from an intellectual point of view) place, his restless spirit began a series of sixty-one lectures at the university, probably as a reaction to the immense annoyance that the situation provoked in him. He gave lectures for six months, several times a week, free of charge. This caused the crowds to flock, from royals to servants, half of them being women, who usually did not have permission to attend either the universities or scientific lectures. They "were finally allowed to listen to *a clever word*". They were amazed and enthusiastic about science, and started to incorporate scientific terms in their vocabulary[43]. During the days when the lectures took place, Berlin descended into such excitement that mounted police officers had to intervene to control the crowds. The auditorium was already filled an hour before Humboldt took the podium. *"The lectures were a portrait of a vivid kaleidoscope of correlations that spanned the entire universe"* (Wulf 2015, 442). The experience was unforgettable—Humboldt guided the audience's spirit from the splendors of the cosmos to the depths of the oceans. Through him, science was democratized and popularized.

Andrea Wulf, author of the most *recent and comprehensive biography of this extraordinary polymath, observes that* "one of Humboldt's greatest achievements had been to make science accessible and popular" *(Wulf 2015, 763).*

42 Over this period of his life, Humboldt spent most of his time at Court, travelling from Palace to Palace, and was only able to work during the night, between midnight and 3 in the morning. Wulf, *The Invention of Nature,* 431.

43 Andrea Wulf narrates a very funny episode, described by the director of the *Singakademie* to Goethe. A lady was so impressed by Humboldt's descriptions of Sirius that she asked her tailor to make the sleeves of her dress "twice the size of Sirius". Ibid., 442.

She adds: "His belief in the free exchange of information, in uniting scientists, and in fostering communication across disciplines are the pillars of science today. His concept of nature as one of global patterns underpins our thinking" (Wulf 2015, 765).

What we intend to demonstrate is that Humboldt's method of assimilating and articulating what he observed was markedly different from the standard of his time—so much so that, as often happens with visionaries, many of his assertions would only be universally accepted much later. This perfectly aligns with the information he shared with Kardec, regarding his origin in a more advanced and distant sphere.

As mentioned earlier, in a period of so many remarkable advances, it is difficult for us not to suspect that many other Spirits were incarnated simultaneously under similar conditions, each contributing to the progress of humanity through their distinct missions.[44]. Our suspicions immediately fall on François Arago (1786-1853), the famous mathematician and astronomer, identified by Humboldt as the Spirit who offered him his hand on the way back to their spiritual homeland[45]. In life, Alexander and François were the best friends, "conjoined twins"[46], according to Humboldt (Wulf 2015, 521). Arago was the only person he trusted unconditionally. They had fiery discussions that did not always end well, but their grievances never lasted[47]. Ac-

44 Despite being little known today, in his day no one equaled Arago in knowledge or intellectual dexterity; he was almost unanimously recognized by his peers as the most influential scholar of his time.

45 "'Have you seen Arago again, after you returned to the spirits' world?' 'It was him who reached out to me when I left your world'". Kardec, *The Spiritist Review* - 1859, 279.

46 Moreover, there were several figures that Humboldt identified as his twin souls, notably Charles Darwin himself, despite being forty years Darwin' senior. Wulf, *The Invention of Nature*, 521.

47 Whenever they were not physically close, they would write to each other. Their letters were published in 1907: *Correspondance d'Alexandre de Humboldt avec François Arago* (1809-1853). The work is 400 pages long, and comprises more than three decades of exchanged mail.

cording to Arago himself, the connection between the two "lasted over forty years without a single cloud ever having troubled it." (Chisholm 1911, 312)

It is worth recalling that François Arago was among the Spirits who collaborated in the Spiritist Codification. His message *"Signs of the Times"* can be found in *Genesis* (Kardec 2011, 411). As a collaborator of the Spirit of Truth, whether or not he was closely connected to this world, it seems certain that he was also a superior Spirit, a divine messenger who came with the mission of contributing to the progress of humankind. This affinity helps explain why Humboldt and Arago were so closely linked when they encountered one another in the same earthly struggles. Great souls naturally resonate with one another, which is why *we find so many convergences between them:* "The sympathy attracting one spirit to another is the result of the perfect harmony of their predispositions and instincts, [...] (of) equal degree of elevation" *(Kardec* 2020, 144).

Moreover, solidarity is a universal law:

> "The entire universe is subject to the law of solidarity. The worlds lost in the depths of the ether, the stars which, at millions of leagues apart, intersect their silvery rays, know each other, call each other, and answer one another. [...] A human soul can only truly progress by living in collective life, working for the benefit of all. [...] Among evolved souls, the feeling of solidarity becomes intense enough to transform into perpetual communion with all beings and with God" *(Denis 2019, 30–33).*

By subjecting themselves to the adversities of material life on an inferior planet, Humboldt and other elevated Spirits voluntarily submit to the beautiful law of universal solidarity, in accordance with the wise designs of Providence. They reincarnate in backward worlds to assist in their moral and intellectual advancement while enriching their own experience and understanding. Nothing is in vain; nothing is futile.

Some earthly commentators have suggested that Humboldt's *Cosmos* is a universe without God, since the word *"God"* rarely appears throughout his vast body of work.[48]. It doesn't seem right, however, to say that the *Cosmos* that triggered more commissions than Goethe's masterpiece, *Faust*[49], was effectively a cosmos without God. It certainly was a cosmos without the God of religions, the anthropomorphic entity conceived by humans, but not without the God that Humboldt objectively venerated through his work.

> Eight years and eight months after Humboldt's passing, Kardec affirmed *that* "God per se does not appear, but is affirmed through God's works" (Kardec 2011, 62). He also wrote: *"Looking around oneself at the wor*ks of Nature—observing the foresight, the wisdom, and the harmony that preside over all things—one realizes that there is not one of them that does not surpass the highest reach of the human mind" (Kardec 2011, 60).
>
> To this, Léon Denis adds:
>
> "Do not seek God in temples of stone and marble [...] but in the eternal temple of Nature instead, in the spectacle offered by the worlds traveling the infinite expanse of space; in the splendors of life which flourish upon their surfaces; in the view of varied hori-

48 *Cosmo* came to be considered a blasphemous book by a German church, which accused Humboldt of having made a pact with the Devil. Wulf, *The Invention of* Nature, 569.

49 More than 20,000 copies of the German edition were sold in the first few months alone. When the second volume was published, in 1847, bribes were offered and book quotas for booksellers were intercepted and diverted by agents who wanted to supply their desperate customers. Wulf, *The Invention of Nature,* 559.

> zons—plains, valleys, mountains, and seas—such as we have in our earthly dwelling. Everywhere, under the light of day or the starry cloak of night, on the edge of tumultuous oceans or in the solitude of forests, if you know how to withdraw yourself into an inner retreat, you will hear the voices of Nature and the subtle teachings it whispers into the ears of those who venture to penetrate its recesses and study its mysteries" (Denis 2019, 14).

He also remarks:

> "The pure soul communicates with the whole of Nature; it is inebriated with the infinite splendors of the Creator's works. The stars in the sky, the flowers in the meadow, the murmur of the running stream, the variety of earthly landscapes, the fleeting horizons of the sea, the serenity of deep space—absolutely everything speaks a harmonious language to it" (Denis 2019, 33).

From an identical perspective, Camille Flammarion underscores the importance of the experience of *fruition*—an experience that is not only intellectual but also aesthetic—arising from the contemplation of Nature as a complement to the knowledge obtained through reason and intelligence. He writes:

> "To the eyes of the soul, it is pleasing to fall in love with the celestial radiation which is abundant in all Nature. Here, it is no longer the discussion, but the contemplation gathered from the light and life resplendent in the atmosphere, that shines in the chromatism of the flowers and in their nuances, that circulates in the foliage of the woods and envelops the innumerable throbbing beings in the bosom of Nature in a universal kiss" (Flammarion 1987, 378).

In constructing his body of knowledge, Humboldt assimilated both subjective experiences—arising from contemplation—and objective experiences—derived from records and measurements grounded in observation. He seems to embody one of those refined souls described by Denis: continually amazed and enchanted by the beauty of Nature, ecstatic, delighting in it as much as he studied it.

At times, he must have resembled a child discovering the world for the first time—lying in a hammock fastened between palm trees, at night, in the heart of the jungle, sheltered beneath a canopy of vines and leaves illuminated by the campfire, under the heavy tropical rain. Surrounded by white smoke spiraling into the sky, he would exalt the sublimity of the moment while describing the Orinoco River—the largest in South America—as *"a blanket of humidity, suspended on its riverbed,"* its dark surface reflecting the constellations of the southern hemisphere, the rainbow halos encircling the moon, the shimmering arches over the great rapids.

Perhaps, for him, these were truly landscapes never seen before—for he had never been incarnated here. There was no parallel between all he once knew and the world he now visited.[50]

From the information that he himself provided to Kardec, we understand that he was in fact a new student. Everything was an exciting and challenging novelty for him on Earth, which left his mind in an uproar, thirsty for knowledge.[51] In his world of origin, there was no sun, and

50 There is, in his biography, a delightful detail, which in our opinion portrays well his enchantment by nature: Humboldt created an instrument to be able to measure the "blueness of the sky", the *cyanometer.* See Wulf *The Invention of Nature,* 590.

51 He went so far as to assure Kardec that certain sciences were totally unknown to him: "...what you have just asked me has no relationship with all that I was able to learn in my existences prior to this one that I have just left, so different from the others. Astronomy, for example, was a completely new science to me." Kardec, *The Spiritist Review - 1859,* 280.

luminosity obeyed different principles (Kardec 2016, 278). Perhaps this explains why Humboldt's last words referred to the *"glorious sunbeams"* that entered his room, as if they were *"calling Earth to the Heavens!"* (Wulf 2015, 634). He was, in truth, a kind of extraterrestrial, suffering from what Léon Denis called the *researcher's vertigo*—that reverent dizziness before the immensity of divine creation. Despite his vast experience and his unequivocal intellectual progress, he remained perpetually astonished before the Divine Majesty, which continuously surprised and seduced him, revealing a new sanctuary of Creation—infinitely diverse, never contradictory, and never repetitive.

As Kardec observes in *Genesis*:

> "Nature has never contradicted itself. The emblem of the universe has only one motto: UNITY - DIVERSITY. Ascending the scale of worlds, unity—both in harmony and in creation—is found at the same time that an infinite diversity is found in the immense flowerbed of the stars. Traversing the degrees of life, from the least of beings up to God, the grand law of continuity is recognized" (Kardec 2011, 120). He continues: "May your studies be applied to the beings that soar through the air; may they descend to the violet growing in the woods; may they break open the depths of the ocean. In everything and everywhere you will read this universal truth: all-powerful Nature acts according to places, times, and circumstances. It is one in its overall harmony, but multiple in its productions" (Kardec 2011, 145).

Like other advanced souls, Humboldt grasped this law of unity within diversity and sought to encompass it in his work and thought. Whether speaking of the "web of life" or the "cheering breath", whatever he revered or before which he bowed, he perceived himself as standing before something far greater than most beings could comprehend. No human description could convey such splendor. It does not seem that he sought the God of men, but rather that he pursued—and ultimately found—a greater order that governs all things: a harmony that connects everything that exists, a logic, a reason for being that became the central quest of his entire existence.

When we read about his fascination around volcanoes[52], about how bewitched he felt when, at the top of the world, on top of a mountain, on the edge of a gorge, his soul, touched, moved even higher, we cannot help thinking about the image created by Allan Kardec of *Men on the Top of the Mountain.*[53] His vision of the nature of our world resembled that of a traveler standing at a mountaintop—gazing from above with an all-encompassing perspective upon a gigantic puzzle, in which every minute piece fits harmoniously within the whole, forming a perpetual interrelationship, an intricate fabric in ceaseless motion (Wulf 2015, 560).

We conclude this article by quoting once again Léon Denis, who masterfully synthesized the relationship between scientific inquiry into the material world and the recognition of a supreme power—the unity within which all diversity is integrated into a framework of perfection:

52 Andrea Wulf describes, with a touch of humor, an episode between Humboldt and Goethe, which demonstrates the fascination of the former with volcanoes. His obsession with the subject led him to investigate them as much as he could and to make science overcome the limitation of only knowing Etna and Vesuvius, the only active ones in Europe. This situation would lead Goethe to play with him, in a letter in which the poet introduced him a female friend: "since you belong to the naturalists who believe that everything was created by volcanoes, I'm sending you a female volcano who completely scorches and burns whatever is left." Wulf, *The Invention of nature,* 191-2.

53 "Dematerialized spirits are like the man on the mountain: space and length of time do not exist for them. However, the extent and penetration of their sight are proportional to their purification and their level in the spirit hierarchy. In comparison to low order spirits, they are like persons armed with powerful telescopes alongside those who have only their naked eyes. Among the latter, the range of sight is limited (...)" Kardec, *Genesis,* 367-8.

"All the researches, all the works of contemporary science, concur to demonstrate the action of natural laws, which a supreme law connects and encompasses in order to form the universal harmony. By this law, a sovereign intelligence is revealed as the very reason of all things: a conscious reason, a universal unity toward which all relations converge, connect, and merge; and where all beings come to draw strength, light, and life—the absolute and perfect Being, immutable foundation and eternal source of all science, truth, and wisdom, of all love." *(Denis 2019, 8)*

Bibliography

CHISHOLM, Hugh (editor). "Arago, Dominique François Jean" in *Encyclopædia Britannica* - 11th ed. Cambridge: Cambridge University Press, 1911.

DENIS, Léon. *The Big Enigma: God and the Universe.* Translated by Helton M. Monteiro. New York: United States Spiritist Council, 2019, Kindle edition.

FLAMMARION, Camille. *Deus na Natureza* [God in Nature]. Rio de Janeiro: FEB, 1987.

KARDEC, Allan. "Family Conversations from Beyond the Grave: Mr. Humboldt" in *The Spiritist Review - 1859: Journal of Psychological Studies.* Translated by Luiz Cheim. New York: United States Spiritist Council, 2016.

KARDEC, Allan. *Genesis - Miracles and Predictions According to Spiritism.* Translated by Darrel W. Kimble and Ily Reis. Brasilia: International Spiritist Council, 2011, Kindle edition.

KARDEC, Allan. *The Spirits' Book: The Principles of Spiritism.* Translated by Nicole Alves - 3rd rev. ed. - New York: United States Spiritist Council, 2020, Kindle edition.

WULF, Andrea. *The Invention of Nature: Alexander von Humboldt's new world.* New York: Alfred A. Knopf, 2015, E-book.

Simão Pedro de Lima is a lawyer and university professor. He holds degrees in Law, Administration, and History, as well as postgraduate qualifications in Modern and Contemporary History, Civil Law, and Business Management. He earned his master's degree in Higher Education, with concentrations in Didactics of Higher Education and Organizational Management. In the Spiritist movement, he is a member of the Spiritist Society Casa do Caminho, in Patrocínio, Minas Gerais, Brazil, where he collaborates in both administrative and doctrinal activities. He is the author of *Viver Melhor: uma abordagem espírita para a vida em sociedade* (Living Better: A Spiritist Approach to Life in Society), published by the Spiritist Federation of the State of Goiás (FEEGO).

A PHILOSOPHICAL PERSPECTIVE ON THE EXISTENCE OF GOD

SIMÃO PEDRO LIMA

INTRODUCTION

God, one of the most spoken words in the world, in many situations, either good or bad. The concept of the existence of God is present in people's ideas, but how can we feel, understand it? Cardozo (1976)[54], in a poem called "Where is God?" says in the first stanza:

> "Where is God? The scientist asks,
> No one has ever seen Him. Who is He?
> The materialist rushes to answer:
> God is only an invention of faith."

"God is only an invention of faith." This statement reveals that the inquiry about God often arises within a religious framework. Since immemorial times, religion has been responsible for speaking about God. Typically, such discussions are devotional in nature, following one or another current of classical theology as applied to specific religions.

54 Cited in the booklet PBDE (Basic Program of Spiritism), edited by the Spiritist Center Luz Eterna, from Curitiba - PR, volume I (1981, 51)

However, God can also be understood through other approaches beyond classical theology. Philosophy is one of these alternative paths. From a philosophical perspective, the approach takes a route that differs from the devotional one. Instead of relying on the premises of classical theology—which studies divine realities in the light of *revelation*—philosophy seeks to understand God through the rational prism. This constitutes what is known as philosophical theology.

Mondim (1997, 13), speaking about philosophical theology, explains:

> "Philosophical theology is the rational study of God—that is, it is the study of the existence, nature, attributes, and operations of God, insofar as these can be apprehended by human intelligence when reflecting upon the phenomena (all phenomena) that we can experience in this world."

Mondim adds that, in the sphere of thought of Scholasticism[55], the material object of philosophical theology is God and the formal object is the rational reflection on God. By this thought, philosophical theology seeks to understand God by strengthening relations with the philosophy of religion and metaphysics.

Within the same philosophical framework, theodicy—a term whose etymology conveys the idea of the *"justification of God"*—also studies God through the prism of reason.

Rather than approaching the divine through the classical theological lens of *revelation* (religion), theodicy seeks a

55 Theological-philosophical system emerged in the 13th century that sought to coordinate philosophy and theology, aligning natural knowledge to revealed knowledge (reason and faith). Aristotelian syllogism was the form of reasoning. It lasted until the end of the 18th century.

rational path for understanding the idea of God.

According to Santos (1964, p. 298),

> "Theodicy is a rational science based on the natural resources of human intelligence."

NATURE OF GOD

According to Santos, within the field of theodicy, the idea of God encompasses absolute essence, perfect existence, and universal causality.

The notion of absolute existence asserts that God exists in and of Itself, independent of any cause. The concept of perfect existence means that God contains in Its own nature the fullness of perfection. Finally, universal causality refers to the idea that God is the reason for being and the primary cause of everything that exists.

Jesus, the supreme model of religious thought, also presented a philosophical (metaphysical) conception for understanding God. In His dialogue with the Samaritan woman, recorded by the evangelist John (4:21), Jesus addresses a theological dispute that had long divided Jews and Samaritans. He says to the woman:

> "Woman, believe me, a time is coming when you will worship the Father neither on this mountain nor in Jerusalem."

The Jews believed that God could only be worshiped in the temple on Mount Zion, while the Samaritans claimed that the true place of worship was Mount Gerizim. This disagreement created great tension, as each group sought to determine the correct way and place to worship God.

Later in the conversation, in John 4:24, Jesus reveals the transcendent nature of God:

> "God is Spirit, and His worshipers must worship in spirit and in truth."

Here, Jesus teaches that God transcends human religious conceptions and cannot be confined to the institutions or rituals of any one people. In this passage, He presents a vision of divine immanence—God present in the personal feeling of faith, not bound by human rules or religious structures.

At that time, Judaism described God as a powerful Lord (*El Shaddai*), the Lord of Hosts (*Yahweh Sabaoth*), an energetic and punitive being whose worship was marked by fear. Jesus, however, transformed this perception by calling God Father (*Abba*), an affectionate term meaning "Daddy." By doing so, He revealed a new understanding of the Divine—one of love, justice, and tenderness, not domination and fear.

In Luke 11:11–13, Jesus declares:

> "Which of you fathers, if your son asks for a fish, will give him a snake instead? Or if he asks for an egg, will give him a scorpion? If you then, though you are evil, know how to give good gifts to your children, how much more will your Father in heaven give the Holy Spirit to those who ask Him!"

Through these words, Jesus reveals the abstract yet benevolent nature of God, whose essence manifests through goodness and justice. He moves from the known ("you, who are imperfect humans") to the unknown ("your Father in Heaven") to demonstrate, by analogy, how divine goodness infinitely surpasses human imperfection. This is the meaning of His statement to the Samaritan woman: "God is Spirit."

Spiritism, one of whose threefold aspects is philosophy (along with science and religion), presents a similar view in its study of God. It also addresses the ideas of absolute essence, perfect existence, and universal causality.

In The Spirits' Book, Kardec (2006, 71) asked the Spirits, in the very first question: "What is God?"

To which they answered: "God is the Supreme Intelligence, the first cause of all things."

The formulation of this question already demonstrates Kardec's philosophical rigor. Notably, he asked "what is" rather than "who is"—avoiding the anthropomorphic conception of God common in religions. By using "what," he pointed to the transcendent nature of the Divine.

The Spirits' answer reflects the very principles elaborated by theodicy: God's absolute essence as "the Supreme Intelligence of the universe," and His universal causality as "the first cause of all things." God is both uncaused cause and source of all existence.

The philosophical study of God—its nature, attributes, and evidences—invites human beings to perceive and feel the Divine more deeply. The definition given by the Spirits reveals both God's immanence and transcendence:

God is immanent, present in the universe and in all living beings, yet transcendent, distinct from and independent of creation. However, this immanence must not be mistaken for pantheism, which identifies God with the universe. As clarified in The Spirits' Book (Kardec 2006, 75, question 14), if pantheism were true, "God would not be God, because the work of creation would be an effect and not the cause; God cannot be both the cause and the effect."

Thus, the Divine immanence does not exclude transcendence. God remains absolutely independent of the universe and reigns sovereign over all things. From the study of God's nature, evidence, and attributes, it follows that God possesses autonomous intelligence, freedom, and perfection—the First Cause, the Uncreated, the Absolute Good.

As Jesus declared to the young man who called Him "Good Master" (Mark 10:18):

"Why do you call me good? No one is good—except God alone."

Finally, Santos (1964, 298) summarizes that through theodicy, we seek "to know the nature, the attributes, and the relations between God and the universe." Thus, according to him, a philosophical study of God unfolds in three dimensions:

1. The existence of God;
2. The attributes of God;
3. The relations between God and the world.

EXISTENCE OF GOD

Regarding the existence of God, Kardec (2006, p. 72) asked the Spirits:

> "Where can the proof of God's existence be found?"
>
> And they replied:
>
> "In a premise that is applied in science: there is no effect without a cause. Investigate the cause of anything that is not the work of human beings, and reason shall provide the answer."
>
> Kardec then adds:
>
> "To believe in God, simply observe the works of creation. The universe exists; therefore, there is a cause.

> Doubting the existence of God would be to deny that every effect has a cause and to presume that something could be created from nothing."

Through the philosophical-Spiritist lens, it is clear that the idea of God does not arise from *revelation* or from religious dogma, but from the rational search for the justification of God's existence. In other words, the philosophical-Spiritist reasoning seeks a rational foundation for the existence of God.

According to Santos (1964, p. 300),

> "Every evidence of God is metaphysical, since God's existence is not an object of intuitive apprehension and can only be demonstrated in the light of metaphysical principles."

Didactically, we may say that the evidences for God's existence can be divided into metaphysical and moral categories.

From the metaphysical standpoint, Santos (1964, pp. 300–301) highlights four fundamental points:

1. The existence of the world;
2. The existence of motion;
3. The existence of life;
4. The existence of order in the universe.

The existence of the world and of motion is indisputable—and it would be illogical to suppose that the planet exists by itself or by mere chance. A planet that obeys physical laws of rotation and revolution, that sustains a breathable atmosphere—all coordinated by accident? If that were the case, it would be an *intelligent accident*, and thus, not an accident at all.

The existence of life, for some, is also attributed to chance. Yet if chance could not even create a planet, how could it create life? Life is too well-organized, too perfect. Only a Supreme Intelligence, uncreated, could bring life into being. Life is not a product of the universe—it is its expression. As Mota Júnior (1998, p. 40) aptly wrote:

> "Everything happens as if the phenomena of macroscopic and microscopic scales, notably in the quantum realm, manifest an order that, in itself, reflects a form of intelligence, which is not the result of chance."

The existence of order in the universe further confirms this reasoning: everything functions in perfect balance. Solar systems and galaxies—billions of them—move in intelligent harmony. Such order must have a guiding reason, a cause preceding all causes: an Uncreated Cause, which is God.

As Mota Júnior (1998, p. 41) observes:

> "The image of order is found everywhere, whether in the invisible realm described by quantum theory or in the visible, particularly as revealed by the theory of deterministic chaos, according to which there is a deep order beneath the apparent chaos of phenomena—from the movement of smoke to the evolution of galactic superclusters. This order has given rise to intelligent beings who now reason about themselves."

From the moral standpoint, Santos (1964, pp. 301–302) points to several evidences for God's existence:

a) the existence of the moral law;

b) the principles of merit and demerit;

c) universal consent;

d) the aspirations of the human soul;

e) mystical experience.

The moral law does not originate in the physical world nor in society; it is something intrinsic to the human being. Kardec (2006, p. 363) addresses this when he asks the Spirits:

> "Where is God's law written?"
>
> They answer:
>
> "In the conscience."
>
> This expresses the inner sense of duty that arises within the human soul—the spiritual being incarnated in humanity.

Regarding merit and demerit, Santos (1964, p. 302) affirms:

> "The principle of merit and demerit exists, and our spirit conceives it as a necessary complement to the principle of duty."

He adds that this principle does not originate in the physical world nor from mere intellectual reflection; rather, it presupposes "the absolute guarantee of a perfect sanction appropriate to the moral law, implying the existence of a real and absolute cause—God."

Kardec (2006, p. 110), in *Heaven and Hell*, conveys a similar idea. In the "Penal Code of Future Life," item 8 reads:

> "The justice of God being infinite, an exact account is kept, for each soul, of the good and the evil done by it in the course of its earthly life. No evil deed, no evil thought, however slight, fails to produce its own appropriate correction; but also, no good deed, however minute, no right feeling, however fleeting, no vir-

> tuous aspiration, however faint, is ever overlooked or remains sterile. Even for the most depraved spirits, these are the seeds of reformation and progress."

Hence, this principle of merit and demerit is inherent in human nature and points to the existence of a Divine Intelligence.

As for universal consent, Santos (1964, p. 301) states:

> "The idea of God is neither the prerogative of philosophers or scientists, nor a modern concept, nor a notion confined to Western civilization."

Rather, it is a universal idea, present in all peoples and cultures, throughout all ages—sometimes expressed as myth, sometimes as religious sentiment, and at times as philosophical or scientific reflection.

Kardec (2006, p. 72) anticipated this reasoning in *The Spirits' Book*, question no. 5:

> "What inference can be drawn from the innate perception possessed by all of humanity concerning God's existence?"
>
> The Spirits replied:
>
> "That God exists; for where would this idea come from if there were no real basis? Once again, this is a corollary of the principle that there can be no effect without a cause."

Kardec then deepens the inquiry (question no. 6):

> "Could our intuitive sense of God's existence simply be the result of education and the product of acquired ideas?"
>
> The Spirits respond:
>
> "If such were the case, how could this intuitive sense

be retained by primitive peoples?"

Kardec concludes:

"If the sentiment of the existence of a Supreme Being were solely the result of education, it would not be universal; it would exist, like all acquired knowledge, only in the minds of those who had received such instruction."

Armstrong (1994, p. 9) echoes this perspective:

"There is reason to affirm that *Homo sapiens* is also *Homo religiosus*. Men and women began to worship gods as soon as they became recognizably human."

Armstrong (1994, p. 9) adds:

"Religions and works of art were created at the same time. That was not merely because people wished to appease powerful forces; these primitive faiths expressed the perplexity and mystery that have always been an essential component of the human experience of this beautiful yet terrifying world. Like art, religion was an attempt to find meaning and value in life despite the suffering inherent to the flesh."

Concerning the aspirations of the human soul—another moral evidence of God's existence—this refers to humanity's innate yearning for what transcends material limitations. The soul longs for something beyond matter, a natural consequence of the inner sentiment previously mentioned.

In the words of Santos (1964, p. 302):

"It is the sum of aspirations that leads the human being to seek, beyond finite beings, an infinite, perfect, and absolute Being, in whom one may find complete satisfaction of one's tendencies toward truth, beauty,

> and goodness. This yearning exists in every human creature and appears with greater prominence in the purest, freest, and most intelligent souls."

Regarding mystical experience as evidence of God's existence, it may be defined as an intimate and transformative encounter between creature and Creator—an experience that profoundly alters one's existential perception and cannot be explained without divine intervention. As Santos (1964, p. 302) notes:

> "It is the sign of an intuitive identity that can only be explained by the existence of a real Being, with whom the mystics believe they are in communication."

Throughout history, countless individuals have lived such experiences—among them Paul of Tarsus, Francis of Assisi, Teresa of Ávila, and John of the Cross. Would all these individuals, whose lives were dramatically transformed, have been deceived by illusion? Certainly not.

In summary, regarding the evidences of God's existence, whether metaphysical or moral, Kardec concludes (*The Spirits' Book*, 2006, p. 73) by asking the Spirits (question no. 9):

> "Where may we see, in the first cause of all things, a supreme intelligence superior to all other intelligences?"
>
> The Spirits wisely replied:
>
> "There is a proverb that dictates, 'The worker is known by his or her work.' Look, then, at the work, and you will find the author. Pride is what creates skeptics. Arrogant human beings want nothing above them, which is why they are called strong-minded. Pitiful beings! Just one breath from God would obliterate them."

Kardec then concludes with a synthesis of remarkable lucidity:

> "We evaluate the power of intelligence by its works. As no human being could create that which is produced by nature, the first cause must be superior to humankind. Regardless of the wonders accomplished by humanity, human intelligence itself has a cause; and the greater the results achieved, the greater must be the cause of which they are the effect. It is this Supreme Intelligence that is the first cause of all things, whatever name humanity may bestow upon it."

ATTRIBUTES OF DIVINITY

Another philosophical dimension in the study of God's existence concerns the attributes of Divinity. At this stage, the objective is no longer to seek evidence of existence, but rather to understand God through the analysis of divine attributes – the very qualities without which God would not be God. This constitutes one of the central themes of philosophical theodicy.

According to Santos (1964, p. 303):

> "As effects always bear certain similarities to the cause that produced them, our knowledge of the divine nature is, without a doubt, real. Nevertheless, it remains incomplete and imperfect, since something can only be perfectly known when considered in itself. Because God is infinite and absolutely perfect, while our intelligence is relative and limited, we shall never grasp divine nature in the fullness of its attributes."

Kardec (2006, p. 74) anticipated this philosophical

reasoning when he asked the Spirits, in question no. 10 of *The Spirits' Book*:

> "Is humanity capable of comprehending the essential nature of God?"
>
> And the Spirits replied:
>
> "No, human beings lack the sense required to comprehend it."

This "no" does not represent a prohibition, but rather a factual impossibility. When the Spirits say that humanity lacks the "sense" necessary to comprehend God, they mean that human beings have not yet developed the faculties required for such understanding.

Kardec then advances his questioning (question no. 11):

> "Will humans ever be able to understand the mystery of Divinity?" The answer was:
>
> "Humans will see and understand God when their spirits are no longer obscured by matter, and when they have come closer to perfection."

This statement reflects the evolutionary nature of the human spirit, which is, so to speak, still in the infancy of its spiritual development. As humanity progresses—both intellectually and morally—it will achieve a clearer and fairer conception of Divinity, although it will still fall short of fully comprehending the Absolute.

Kardec continues (question no. 12):

> "If we cannot comprehend the essential nature of God, can we at least grasp an idea of some of God's perfections?"

The Spirits respond:

> "Yes, some of them. Human beings understand them better as they rise above matter. They catch glimpses of them through thought."

In harmony with Kardec's reasoning, Santos (1964, pp. 304–305) categorizes God's attributes into three groups:

1. Entitative attributes: simplicity, infinity, unity, immensity, immutability, and eternity.
2. Operational attributes: intelligence and will.
3. Moral attributes: wisdom, goodness, and justice.

Kardec (2006, p. 74–75) presented several of these same divine attributes in *The Spirits' Book* (question no. 13), describing God as:

> "Eternal, infinite, unchangeable, immaterial, unique, all-powerful, supremely just and good."

> The Spirits, responding to Kardec, clarified:

> "From your point of view, yes, because you think you sum up everything in those terms. However, you must understand that there are things which transcend even the most advanced human intelligence, and which your language cannot express. Reason tells you that God must possess all these qualities in the supreme degree; for if any of them were lacking, or were not possessed to an infinite degree, the Creator would not be superior to all things, and thus would not be God. To be above all things, God must have no variations and no conceivable imperfections."

Thus, the Spirits affirm that Kardec's description is didactic, framed from a human perspective. God indeed possesses these attributes—and infinitely more that human language is incapable of expressing.

What stands out in this reply is the Spirits' insistence that God has no variations and no human imperfections. Historically, people have often attributed human passions to God, as seen in the Book of Exodus (Almeida, 1975, p. 77), where God is portrayed as jealous, wrathful, and punitive—"visiting the iniquity of the fathers upon the children unto the third and fourth generation of them that hate Me."

Clearly, such traits cannot belong to the Divine. These are human projections—attributes of human nature ascribed to God. As Feuerbach (1988, p. 55) insightfully states:

> "As a person thinks, so is their God. The consciousness of God is the consciousness that humans have of themselves; the knowledge of God and the knowledge of humankind are one and the same. By knowing God, one knows humanity; and by knowing humanity, one knows its God."

Though Feuerbach's view arises from a materialist and humanist philosophy, his observation reveals a psychological truth: humanity tends to idealize God according to its own moral and intellectual limitations.

In this regard, Mondin (1997, p. 297) writes:

> "The Absolute is a name frequently given to God. By this we mean that God is *solutus*, 'free': unconditioned, unbound by any limitations."

The Spirits, therefore, affirm that human beings are still too undeveloped to comprehend God's intimate nature. Kardec's questions thus serve as didactic instruments, guiding reflection through attributes accessible to human understanding.

Among them, the first is that "God is eternal", which includes the notion of infinity. God has neither beginning nor end. Kardec (2006, p. 75) explains:

> "If God had a beginning, God would either have sprung from nothing, or have been created by a being that existed before. Thus, we are led inevitably to the idea of infinity and eternity."

The second attribute is that "God is unchangeable". Were God subject to change, the universe would lose order and stability. As Santos (1964, p. 304) notes:

> "Every change implies either progress or decline. Only imperfect beings change and transform."
>
> Hence, being absolute perfection, God cannot be subject to change.

The third attribute: "God is immaterial." Since matter is subject to transformation, an immutable God cannot be composed of matter.

The fourth: "God is unique." If there were more than one God, Kardec explains,

> "There would be neither unity in the plans of the universe, nor harmony in its organization."

Two gods, equal in perfection, would be indistinguishable; if they differed, neither would be perfect.

The fifth attribute: "God is all-powerful." Being unique implies possessing all power. Were it otherwise, something would exist equal or superior to God—an absurdity, since the work cannot surpass the author.

Finally, "God is supremely just and good." As Kardec states,

> "The great wisdom of the divine laws is clearly re-

vealed in the smallest and the greatest things. This wisdom makes it impossible to doubt God's justice or goodness."

Here lies the moral evidence of God's existence: the principle of merit and demerit. As Santos (1964, p. 305) summarizes:

> "Possessing absolute holiness, which is the order of love, God acts with infinitely perfect justice—punishing evil and rewarding good."

CONCLUSION

In conclusion, we may affirm that even with all the philosophical, scientific, and theological reasoning available, the understanding of God remains a personal and intimate experience.

At the beginning of this article, the first stanza of a poem by Cardozo (1976) was quoted, as reproduced in the booklet *PBDE – Basic Program of the Spiritist Doctrine*, published by *Centro Espírita Luz Eterna* (Curitiba – PR, vol. I, 1981, p. 51), in the poem entitled *"Where is God?"*. To close this reflection, we reproduce its final stanza:

> "Where I feel God with more beauty,
> In its sublime expression,
>
> Is not in the heart of nature,
> But within my own heart."

This thought aligns with what the Spirits revealed to Kardec in *The Spirits' Book* (question no. 5), that the intuitive sentiment of God's existence within the human soul is, in itself, a proof "that God exists."

Through the path of religion, God is sought through revelation; through the path of science, God is sought through material evidence; through the path of philosophy, God is sought through reason and reflection.

In the Spiritist perspective, these three paths converge without merging. Each preserves its essence, yet together they illuminate a broader and more elevated understanding of the Divine. In this synthesis, God is perceived in His greatness, presence, manifestation, immanence, and transcendence—as the First Cause of all things, the perfect and supreme intelligence of the universe, the Lord of Life.

Bibliography

ALMEIDA, João F. 1975. *A Bíblia Sagrada* (Novo Testamento) - *The Holy Bible* (New Testament). Rio de Janeiro: Imprensa Bíblica Brasileira.

ARMSTRONG, Karen. 1994. *Uma História de Deus. Quatro Milênios de Busca do Judaísmo, Cristianismo e Islamismo - A History of God. The 4.000-year Quest of Judaism, Christianity and Islam.* [Translated by Marcos Santarrita]. São Paulo: Cia das Letras.

CARDOZO, José S. 1976. *Onde Está Deus?- Where is God?* São Paulo: Tempos Novos Ltda.

FEUERBACH, Ludwig. 1988. *A Essência do Cristianismo - The Essence of Christianity.* [Translated by José da Silva Brandão]. Campinas: Papirus.

KARDEC, Allan. *Heaven and Hell or the Divine Justice According to Spiritism.* (USSF/ISC)

KARDEC, Allan. *The Spirits' Book.* (USSF/ISC)

MONDIN, Battista. 1997. *Quem é Deus? Elementos de Teologia Filosófica - Who is God? Elements of Philosophical Theology.* [Translated by José Maria de Almeida]. São Paulo: Paulus.

MOTA JUNIOR, Elizeu F. 1998. *Que é Deus? - Who is God?* Matão: O Clarim.

SANTOS, Theobaldo Miranda. 1964. *Manual de Filosofia - Manual of Philosophy.* São Paulo: Companhia Editora Nacional.

José Raul Teixeira Educator, speaker, and medium; co-founder of the Fraternidade Spiritist Society (Niterói) and of the Spiritist Social Assistance organization "Remanso Fraterno." He holds a Master's and a Ph.D. in Education and a degree in Physics from the Fluminense Federal University, where he is currently a retired professor.

Alessandro Vieira de Paula Member of the Allan Kardec Spiritist Center in Itapetininga, São Paulo (Brazil).

GREATNESS OF GOD

RAUL TEIXEIRA AND
ALESSANDRO VIEIRA DE PAULA

The evolutionary process of the human species culminated in *Homo sapiens*—literally, "the wise human"—approximately 350,000 years ago, reaching modern cognitive and behavioral development about 50,000 years ago.

With the emergence of rational thought—the ability to draw conclusions, reason through arguments, and develop abstractions—human beings began to question the origins of existence: *Where does everything that exists come from?* What is the source of the moon, the sun, the stars, the waters, nature itself, the planet, and humankind?

In the early stages of humanity's intellectual development, primitive conceptions naturally arose, such as polytheistic beliefs, wherein multiple gods were thought to preside over different aspects of nature: a god of the sun, of the rain, of the oceans, and so forth.

As human consciousness evolved, so did these religious ideas. In accordance with the psychological and moral level of that period, humanity first developed the mythological representations of the Greek Olympus and the Roman pantheon, imagining gods who needed to be appeased or flattered through sacrifices—sometimes of animals, sometimes even of humans or plants—so as to secure their favor and avoid divine wrath.

The emergence of Judaism, however, marked a profound shift in human spirituality by introducing the concept of one God, Creator of all things and all beings—a revolutionary step toward a higher understanding of divine unity. From this monotheistic foundation, other religious traditions later developed.

Parallel to this, arose another current of thought: that the universe came into being by chance, and that all existence could be explained by the combination of time and natural laws—gravity, electromagnetism, and the strong and weak nuclear forces—following the great cosmic event known as the Big Bang.

In modern times, these perspectives have grown more complex, giving rise to a continuing intellectual dialogue—and often a tension—between creationist (theistic) and evolutionary (atheistic) schools of thought.

Nevertheless, it must be recognized that Jesus represented a turning point in humanity's understanding of God. He presented the image of a loving Father, Creator of all, who loves each of His children unconditionally—a God liberated from the distortions of religious fanaticism and from the limitations of materialist reductionism.

In the Gospel of John (4:4–30), we find the extraordinary dialogue between Jesus and the Samaritan woman. The Samaritans prayed on Mount Gerizim, while the Jews prayed in the Temple of Jerusalem, on Mount Zion. When the woman asked Jesus which place was right for worship, the Master gave a reply that still echoes through the centuries. He explained that the time would come when true worship would no longer be confined to any specific mountain or place, for the genuine way to worship God is "in spirit and in truth" (*John 4:5–42*).

In this sublime lesson, Jesus revealed that God is everywhere, including within each of us, and that prayer is an act of spiritual communion, not dependent on temples or rituals. Worship is a matter of sincerity, inner transformation, and moral alignment with divine goodness.

What a profound shift in human understanding of God! No longer a partial or tribal deity who favors some and rejects others, but a universal Father who loves all beings equally and unconditionally.

With the advent of Spiritism, the teachings of Jesus concerning God were clarified and expanded—not because the Divine Teacher's message was incomplete, but because human limitation and imperfection had obscured and restricted its true meaning.

In The Spirits' Book, the first of Allan Kardec's Spiritist Codification, in Part I - The Primary Causes, Chapter I, the spiritual instructors present clear and direct concepts to help us understand God as the Supreme Intelligence and First Cause of all things. They also reveal that humanity cannot yet comprehend the intimate nature of the Divine, who is sovereignly just and good.

It is worth noting that several renowned scientists throughout history have openly affirmed their belief in God, including Galileo Galilei, Isaac Newton, Nicolaus Copernicus, and, more recently, the distinguished English astrophysicist Sir James Jeans.

In the light of Spiritism, which explains the divine law of progress, we understand that true comprehension of creation arises from the harmonization between creationism and evolution. Both currents reveal complementary aspects of divine wisdom, for God is the Creator of all things. However, creation did not occur as literally described in Genesis (chapters 1 and 2); that account is a symbolic representation.

God, in divine intelligence, employed the law of evolution as the mechanism of creation—acting simultaneously on the material and spiritual planes—to populate the Earth and the "many other mansions in my Father's house."

From this understanding of God—who created us simple and ignorant, endowed with embryonic spiritual faculties that have been evolving for billions of years through the lower realms of creation (mineral, vegetal, and animal)—we derive the meaning of existence. Thus, our primary efforts must be devoted to the progress of the intellect and of the moral sense.

The knowledge of divine laws, both material and moral, united with noble sentiments, will enable us to discover the Kingdom of God within us, as Jesus proclaimed.

Guided by this faith "in spirit and in truth," we become co-workers in the construction of a regenerated world, spreading and living the message of love and goodness.

It is Jesus who calls us to let our light shine before others, so that they may see our good works and glorify God (*Matthew 5:16*).

Even today, however, there remain skeptical, atheistic, and materialistic individuals, whose faith is shaken and whose hearts suffer in silence. For this reason, we are invited to live the Gospel intensely, so that the small light of our example may illuminate other lives. God often chooses human beings themselves as instruments of divine help to one another.

It is therefore our mission to bring God into our homes—by being good children, spouses, parents, and grandchildren; by practicing patience and compassion toward our most difficult family members. Our love, like a gentle flame, will gradually soften hardened hearts, which will awaken sooner or later, for we are all immortal spirits destined for plenitude, guided by the pedagogical law of reincarnation. After all, God dwells within us.

Let us also carry God into society—into our daily lives, our workplaces, the streets, and the communities we belong to. May our words of kindness and faithfulness, inspired by Christ's teachings, and our serene, gentle, and peaceful actions, demonstrate that God governs all things and that nothing is lost. Evil and error are temporary, while good and truth are eternal.

Wherever we are, may our virtuous and noble actions reveal that God is always with us. No one is forgotten or abandoned, for the infinite love of God embraces every creature.

Some souls are so spiritually ill that they cannot yet perceive that God lives within them, nor feel that they are immersed in the Divine Mind. Such hearts need to perceive the presence of God through the balanced and charitable conduct of others.

Spiritism revives and clarifies the teachings of Jesus, leaving no doubt about Divine Fatherhood. It awakens in us a deep sensitivity, allowing us to recognize, every day, the signature of God in all things, and to feel His presence vibrating within our own souls.

Thus we understand the luminous affirmation of Paul of Tarsus, who wrote:

"For in Him we live and move and have our being." (*Acts 17:28*)

www.ingramcontent.com/pod-product-compliance
Lightning Source LLC
LaVergne TN
LVHW020046110826
845155LV00029B/646
* 9 7 8 1 9 4 8 1 0 9 4 8 2 *